The
Short
Course
Programme

pre-intermediate

...EXPECTATIONS

Matthew Farthing &
Alan Pulverness

First published 1995

Published by MACMILLAN PUBLISHERS LTD
London and Basingstoke

ISBN 0–333–61795–9

Produced by AMR

Printed in Malta by Interprint Limited

A catalogue record for this book is available from the British Library.

ACKNOWLEDGEMENTS

The authors and publishers wish to acknowledge, with thanks, the following photographic sources:

Stuart Boreham Photography pages 4 top left, 4 centre left, 6 top centre left, 6 top centre right, 6 centre far left, 6 centre right, 6 centre far right, 6 bottom left, 6 bottom centre, 6 centre right, 6 bottom right, 8, 13, 16 top left, 16 centre left, 16 bottom right, 17 top, 17 bottom, 24 centre right, 26, 28, 32 centre left, 32 bottom, 33 top, 33 top left, 33 top left, 33 bottom right, 36, 40, 44 top, 46 top far left, 46 top left, 46 top right, 46 top far right, 56, 64 bottom left, 66 centre, 71 bottom right, 72,79 middle; K and J Dodd page 57; Greg Evans International pages 4 top centre, 4 centre right, 4 bottom right, 6 top far right, 6 centre left, 16 top, 16 top right, 16 centre right, 16 bottom left, 16 bottom right, 17 centre, 24 top centre, 24 centre left, 31 bottom left, 32 top, 32 centre right, 33 centre right, 33 top left, 33 centre right, 40 top left, 44 centre, 44 bottom, 46 centre far left, 46 centre left, 46 bottom left, 46 bottom right, 46 bottom far right, 47 top, 64 top left, 66 top left, 66 top centre, 66 top right, 66 centre right, 66 centre left; Sally and Richard Greenhill pages 31 top right, 31 bottom right, 46 bottom centre, 66 centre left, 66 bottom right, 71 top left, 79 centre left; Oxford University pages 18, 79 bottom left; Picturepoint pages 66 bottom left, 71 bottom left; Queen Mary's College Central Studio page 79 centre right; Rex Features Ltd pages 24 top left, 24 top right, 31 top left, 33 bottom right, 33 bottom left; Chris Ridgers page 6 top far left; Tony Stone Worldwide pages 24 bottom right, 33 top right, 64 centre, 66 centre far right; Zefa pages 46 centre far right, 47 bottom, 64 bottom right, 71 top right, 79 top.

Cover poster 'The West-End is awakening' reproduced by courtesy of The London Transport Museum.

The authors and publishers would also like to thank the Public Affairs Office, South West Trains, for permission to reproduce the British Rail materials on page 28.

The publishers have made every effort to trace copyright holders, but if they have inadvertently overlooked any they will be pleased to make the necessary arrangements at the first opportunity.

Illustrations by David Birdsall, Josephine Blake, Phillip Burrows, Jon Davis, Graham Cameron Illustration, Jane Jones, Bill Piggins, Jane Spencer, Charles Whelon

CONTENTS

INTRODUCTION

Welcome to **Expectations**. This book is for you, to help you to learn English and practise English while you are in Britain. **Expectations** is the first book in *The Short Course Programme*: Expectations, Impressions, Observations and Reflections.

What is the book about?

- It is a language course that helps you to use English in Britain.

Who is it for?

- Anyone with a basic level of English.

How long is the course?

- The course can last for anything from 60 to 100 hours.

What is in the book?

- There are four units that follow your time in Britain:
    Unit 1 is called 'Asking Questions'
    Unit 2 is called 'Getting About'
    Unit 3 is called 'Meeting People'
    Unit 4 is called 'Planning Ahead'.

What is in each unit?

- Each unit has:
    - four **sections** (eight pages) to help you with the language you need to enjoy your stay in Britain
    - two pages to help you build the **vocabulary** that you need every day
    - two pages for a project that you do **'out of class'** and **pronunciation** work
    - two pages of basic English **grammar** points and exercises
    - two pages to help you think about how you are learning and **review** the unit.
    In addition, each unit has two pages of supplementary grammar practice exercises for you to do on your own or as homework.

What is the unit review?

- This is when you think about what you are learning and how you are learning. It is important for you to think about your own strengths and weaknesses. It is also important to look forward at the beginning of each unit and to look back at the end. You also have a learner diary at the back of the book to help you follow your own progress.

What is the 'out of class' project?

- This is the time when you take your English outside the classroom and communicate with people in real situations. You prepare the project in small groups and share your results with the rest of the class.

What do I learn outside the classroom?

- You spend more time learning English when you are outside the classroom than you do in lessons. Outside you are listening to English, reading things in English, looking at the images around you and speaking in English. **Expectations** has been carefully written to help you to bring all of these experiences back into the classroom where you can work on your own personal strengths and weaknesses.

Why is it important to think about life in Britain?

- Anyone who is learning English in Britain is interested in life in Britain. You will go on many visits and spend time in shops, restaurants, pubs and places of local interest. All of these experiences will involve English and **Expectations** will help you to understand the close links between the language and the lives of people who speak it.

What skills are covered in Expectations?

- The learning activities involve reading, listening and speaking. There is also space for writing in the course diary.

What is the course diary?

- This is at the back of the book. It is where you write down your ideas about your course. There are two diary pages for each unit. You can keep a record of the language you are learning and how your English is improving from week to week. Each diary section asks you to write down some **action points**. These are statements of what you need to do during the next week. You can also write down new vocabulary, useful expressions and grammar points to remember.

Do I need to know anything else?

- The coursebook will help you to learn, but remember that this is your course.
    Speak as much as you can.
    Don't worry about making mistakes.
    Listen to other people speaking around you – in shops, cafés, etc.
    Watch the television and listen to the radio.
    Look at newspapers and magazines.
    Ask for help when you need it.
    Enjoy the course and make the most of your time in Britain.

Note: The Teacher's Book contains a Word List covering all the words used in the Student's Book. If you would like a copy, ask your teacher.

4

ASKING QUESTIONS

In this unit you will find:

- language practice to help you
    - ask what something is;
    - ask how much something costs;
    - ask what something means;
    - ask where someone comes from;

- vocabulary to help you talk about
    - colours and shapes;
    - countries and nationalities;
    - the time;

- pronunciation work on
    - the alphabet in English;
    - the vowel sounds of English;
    - short forms;

- your 'Out of class' project
    - to collect information about shops, services and restaurants;
    - to compare prices in Britain with other countries;
    - to prepare a poster presentation;

- grammar points to teach you about
    - *wh* questions;
    - *yes/no* questions;
    - questions with *be*;
    - questions with *do* and *does*;
    - question tags.

SECTION 1

WHAT'S THAT?

❶ What are these things and places called in your language? Do you know the words in English?

❷ Match the two groups of pictures.

❸ **Pairwork** Ask and answer questions about the pictures, like this:

Examples

| Questions: | *What* | *is this/that* | *(called)?* |
| | | *are these/those* | |

| Answers: | *I think* | *it's (called) a ....* |
| | | *they're (called) ....s* |

❹ Listen and read. Match the conversations with the pictures.

a
- Excuse me. Is this a phone card?
- Yes, of course it is.
- But it won't go in here.
- Oh, it's the wrong card. You want a blue card for this phone. The green card's for that phone over there.

b
- Hey! Don't you know there's a queue?
- Oh, I'm sorry. Where do I get the 24, then?
- You stand over there, behind all those people.

c
- Good morning. Can I help you?
- Yes. Have you got a map of the city?
- Certainly. This small one is free or there's this large one. It gives you a lot of information about places to go and things to see.

d
- Next, please!
- I'd like a book of stamps, please.
- First or second?
- I'm not sure. They're for letters to Italy.
- Oh, you want first class, then. These orange ones. That'll be £2.50, please.

Unit 1

❺ Pairwork Think of a room in the house where you are living. Choose an object in the room and answer your partner's questions about it.

Examples

Questions:	Vocabulary for answers:
How big ⎫	*quite/very small/large*
What shape ⎬ *is it?*	*round/square/long/flat*
What colour ⎭	*black/blue/brown/green/grey/*
	red/silver/yellow
Is it expensive?	*Yes, it is./No, it isn't.*
What's it for?	*It's for … ./You can … with it.*
Is it a … ?	*Yes, that's right./No, it's a … .*

❻ Listen and write the missing words. Who are the speakers? Where are they?

a '_____ to Bonds Department Store. This is a _____ announcement. There are _____ offers in all departments today. This week only! Hundreds of things at _____ low prices! Look out for the red 'Spring Sale' signs in _____ department. All these 'Spring Sale' items have been in the store at higher _____ for at least two months. And don't _____ that it's our late night shopping night tonight – we're _____ until eight o'clock this evening.'

b • Excuse me. What _____ is the last bus to Northfields?
 • I'm _____ you're too late. The last bus is at 10.30.
 • Oh. Where can I _____ a taxi, then?
 • Over there – where _____ people are queueing – in front of the Tourist Information Centre.
 • Thanks very much.

❼ Listen and answer the questions.

Dialogue A

1 What message do you see when you put in your phone card?
 a Phone now   *b* Call now   *c* Dial now

2 How many units of time are there on a £4 phone card?
 a 14   *b* 40   *c* 400

3 If you want to go on talking when your phone card finishes, do you
 a put another card in?
 b say goodbye very quickly?
 c pay another £4?

Dialogue B

1 If you want to be sure that a letter arrives the next day, do you send it by
 a first class post?
 b second class post?
 c Special Delivery?

2 How much extra does Special Delivery cost?
 a £1.15   *b* £1.50   *c* £1.55

❽ Use these words to complete the signs.
tours   here   shopping   last   early   queue

❾ Pairwork Use the question words to ask about the pictures. Can your partner answer your questions?

Where ...?   When ...?   What time ...?   What ...?

SECTION 2

HOW MUCH IS IT?

❶ Work in pairs and ask each other about these British signs.

- What is the name of the place?
- What kind of business is it?
- What can you get there?
- Have you been there?

❷ Is the sentence true or false? Look at the pictures below and decide.

1 The student is buying a magazine.
2 The shop sells fruit and vegetables.
3 The newsagent sells cigarettes.
4 The student knows how much things cost.
5 The newsagent is helpful.

❸ Now write new sentences to make them all true.

❹ What do you think the student is saying to the newsagent? What do you think the newsagent is saying to the student? Work in pairs and write down their conversation.

❺ Act out their conversation for the rest of the class.

❻ Listen to the recording of their conversation. Write down what they say.

❼ Work in pairs. Choose to be the shopkeeper or the customer. Plan the conversation for the situation below, but don't write it down. Try it with your partner and then act it out for the class.

Shopkeeper
You sell fruit and fruit juice.
Oranges are £1.50 for three.
Apples are 40p each.
Orange juice is £1.80 for a litre.
A large bunch of bananas is £2.20.

Customer
You want to buy three oranges, a bunch of bananas and a carton of orange juice.
You don't know the words 'carton of orange juice'.
You only have five pounds.

❽ Ask each other how much these things cost in Britain and in your own country. Then ask about other things too.

Oranges
Stamps
A bar of chocolate
A local three-minute telephone call
A telephone call to America
A newspaper
A litre of orange juice
An orange juice in a café

> How much do/does ... cost?
> How much is it/that?
> What do/does ... cost?

❾ Money and numbers. Write down what you hear.

❿ Say the following:

1	£2.20	6	£2.02
2	£650	7	£250,000
3	£1.99	8	£0.44
4	£2,500	9	£18.00
5	£5.50	10	£0.80

WHAT DO YOU THINK?

⓫ Read these statements and decide. Compare Britain with your own country.

1 Clothes are cheaper in Britain.
2 Restaurants are more expensive in Britain.
3 The shops are more interesting in Britain.
4 Food is less interesting in Britain.
5 There are more magazines and newspapers in Britain.

SECTION 3

WHAT DOES THAT MEAN?

❶ Look at the pictures. What do you think the student is saying?

A

B

C

D

E

❷ Choose the best question for each picture.

1 What's that called?
2 What does this mean?
3 When do you say this?
4 How do you spell it?
5 What do you mean?

❸ Use questions from Exercise 2 (and your own ideas) to complete the conversations.

1 • When _____?
   • It's what you say when you meet someone for the first time. The two people usually shake hands.
   • What _____?
   • Well, it sounds strange, but the other person says exactly the same thing!

2 • When _____?
   • That's what you say when you meet a friend or someone you know.
   • What _____?
   • Oh, you usually say something like 'Fine, thanks' or 'Not too bad' and then you ask the same question. People don't really want to know how you are – it's just the right thing to say!

3 • How _____?
   • It's double 'c' and double 'm'. But don't worry, lots of native speakers forget the double 'm'!
   • Are _____?
   • No, I'm afraid not. There are some spelling rules, but there are a lot of words that you just have to know.

4 • What _____?
   • Well, it's a telephone directory with the numbers of shops and companies, but everyone calls it 'The Yellow Pages'.
   • How _____?
   • You can either look it up in the ordinary phone book or call 192 – that's Directory Enquiries.

❹ Listen and match the conversations to the pictures.

A

B

C

D

❺ Answer the questions on the tape with information about yourself.

❻ Put the phrases in the box below into three groups with these headings:

Formal
(to people you don't know)

Semi-formal
(to people you don't know very well)

Informal
(to people you know quite well)

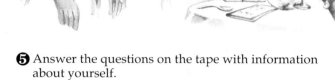

Hello   How do you do?   Hi!   Thank you   Thanks
Certainly   Sure   OK   Pleased to meet you
Good to see you   How nice to see you   What's new?
How are you getting on?   How are things going?
How are you doing?   What are you doing these days?

Can you add any more words/phrases to the three lists?

❼ Complete the following conversation openings:

1 ● How _____ _____ _____? I'm _____
   _____ _____ _____ _____.

   ● How do you do?

2 ● Hello. How _____ _____?

   ● _____ _____ _____. How are you?

3 ● Hi! How _____ _____ _____?

   ● Hi! _____ _____.

11

SECTION 4

WHERE DO YOU COME FROM?

❶ Look at the pictures and write down all the words you think of.

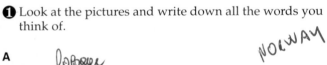

A

lopopie   NORWAY   ITALY

B

18th Century Portraits

C

❷ Work in pairs and compare your lists.

❸ Ask each other: Where do you think the people come from?

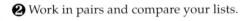

❹ Listen to the conversations and make notes in the boxes below.

	A	B	C	D
Where are they from?				
Nationality(ies)				
Key phrases				

5 How would you say these expressions? Who do you think might be speaking? Who do you think they might be speaking to? Where do you think they might be?

- Ah, so you're from France. Paris?
- And what is your national status exactly, Mr Gregorich?
- Hi, I'm from New York. What about you?
- Where are you from, Peter, if you don't mind my asking?
- So you're from Belfast originally, but you've been living in Brighton for twelve years.
- Which part of India are you from, Indira?
- Are you German, Heinz?
- With a name like Chin Tzu, you must be from the Far East. Whereabouts exactly?
- You look like you've come from another planet dressed like that, Jane. What would your father say?

6 Now listen to the tape and say the expressions again.

7 **Writing** Work in pairs. Choose one of the situations below and write a short conversation. When you have finished, act it out to the rest of the class.

a Two people are sitting at Frankfurt airport waiting for the plane to London. The plane has been delayed for three hours. They are introducing themselves.

b Two people are at a party. They are attending the same language school. This is their first meeting. They are introducing themselves.

c Passport control. The officer wants to know where the traveller has come from and how long s/he plans to stay in the country.

8 Look at the stamps below. They are all from Britain. Look at them carefully and write down five questions about the stamps. Pass your list of questions to someone else.

9 Check the questions. Are they grammatically correct? Can you answer them?

10 **Pairwork** Think of a stamp or a flag from any country. Draw it, but don't show your partner. Now your partner will ask you questions about it and draw what you say. When you have finished, compare your drawings.

| What colour …? |

| What shape …? |

| How big …? |

| … at the top … |

| … under the … |

| … next to the … |

GRAMMAR

LANGUAGE PRACTICE

Question forms

❶ Find the right answers for the questions.

1	Where does she come from?	a	Only five pounds fifty.
2	How much does it cost?	b	At nine thirty.
3	Do you know the number for Directory Enquiries?	c	192.
		d	Just for a few weeks.
4	How long are you staying in Britain?	e	Yes, she's from Recife.
5	What time does the bank open?	f	No, just for a few weeks.
6	When do the British shake hands?	g	When you first meet them.
7	Are you staying in Britain for long?	h	No, it's only five pounds fifty.
8	Is it expensive?	i	She's from Recife.
9	What number do you call for Directory Enquiries?	j	Yes, it's 192.
10	Does Maria come from Brazil?		

❷ The questions and answers below are mixed up. Can you find the conversation?

- Well, I come from Sardinia, but now I live in Rome.
- And are you studying in Britain?
- Is that long enough?
- I'm still a student.
- Not really. I'd like to stay longer.
- How long is your course?
- Yes, I'm trying to improve my English.
- It's just four weeks.
- Where are you from?
- And what do you do there?

❸ Pairwork Complete the questions and use them to interview your partner.

1 What sports _____
   _____?
2 Where _____
   _____play?
3 _____
   _____expensive?
4 _____
   _____special clothes?
5 How often _____
   _____practise?

❹ Use *Which?* or *What?* to complete the questions.

A _____ number bus goes to the city centre?

B _____ time does the film start?

C _____ would you like – the chicken or the beef?

D _____ would you like to order, sir?

LANGUAGE STUDY

GRAMMAR POINTS 1

Wh – questions

Who Where When Why How Which What
Which + noun (e.g. *Which book?*) *What* + noun (e.g.
What time?) *How* + adjective (e.g. *How long?*)
Use these words to ask for information.

Yes/No questions

be have do can could will would
Use these words to ask for a 'Yes/No' answer.

Questions with *be*

To form questions with *be*, put the verb in front of the
subject:

Examples

She is leaving at the end of the month. (When) *is she*
leaving?
They are studying English. (What) *are they* studying?

Questions with *do/does*

To form questions with other verbs, use *do/does*:

Examples

The post office closes at 5.30. What time *does* the post office
close?
They live in London. Where *do* they live?

GRAMMAR POINTS 2

In conversation, you can often give short answers which do
not repeat the main verb or the object.

Short answers for *Yes/No* questions

Repeat the subject. (If the subject is a noun, change it to a
pronoun.)
Repeat the first verb in the question.

Examples

Is it raining?
Yes, *it is.*

Do the students get a lot of homework?
No, *they don't.*

Short questions as answers

Make short questions in the same way as short answers,
putting the verb before the subject.

Examples

It's raining.
Is it?

The students get a lot of homework.
Do they?

Question tags

In conversation, you can also ask the other person to agree
with you by using a question tag. (The tag isn't a real
question – you expect the other person to agree.)

Make question tags in the same way as short questions.
If the sentence is positive, use a negative tag.
If the sentence is negative, use a positive tag.

Examples

It's raining, *isn't it?*
It isn't raining, *is it?*

The students get a lot of homework, *don't they?*
The students don't get a lot of homework, *do they?*

GRAMMAR POINTS 3

There are two *Wh-* question words which are sometimes
confusing.

Which and *What*

Use *Which* when the choice is from a limited number.

Example

Which card can I use in this phone? (the blue one or the
green one)

Use *What* when the choice is from an unlimited number.

Examples

What languages do you speak? (out of all the languages in
the world)
Which language do you speak the best? (out of the
languages which you speak)

GRAMMAR POINTS 4

Sometimes *Wh-* questions ask for information about the
subject and sometimes about the object.

Wh- questions with and without *do*

Use *do/does* when the question word is the <u>object</u>.

Example

SUBJECT   OBJECT
She wants a return ticket.

OBJECT   SUBJECT
What kind of ticket *does* she want?

Don't use *do/does* when the question word is the <u>subject</u>.

Example

SUBJECT
Five students come from Brazil.

SUBJECT
Which students come from Brazil?

VOCABULARY

COLOURS

❶ Look at the picture and write down all of the words you can think of.

❷ Compare your list with someone else's. How many words are the same? How many are new to you?

❸ Write a postcard to a friend, using as many of the words as possible.

❹ What colours can you link to these things? Can you say them?

- danger
- the sun
- grass
- the sky
- the night sky
- dawn

- dusk
- the sea
- earth
- death
- clouds
- snow

❺ ...*ish*, ...*y*, *light and bright*, *dark and deep*. (**Note:** we often put *ish* or *y* on the end of spoken words to mean 'sort of' or 'rather like'. The colour of the sea for example may be described as a *greenish, bluish grey* or a *greeny, bluey grey*.)

Listen to these people. What are they talking about? How do they speak about the colours?

SHAPES

❻ Draw the following shapes.

- a square
- a triangle
- a circle

- a rectangle
- a pentagon
- a hexagon

❼ Draw lines linking these shapes with their words.

1   a pyramid
2   a spiral
3   a cone
4   a cube
5   a cylinder
6   an oval
7   a sphere

A

B

C

D

G

F

E

❽ Work in pairs. Think of an object. Draw it. Now your partner will ask you questions about it and should try to draw what you say. You should only speak about the shape. When you have finished, compare your drawings.

Examples
- a straight line
- a curved line
- then it's got a triangle on top
- is roundish but not an exact circle
- with sharp triangular edges
- cone shaped, like a volcano

COUNTRIES AND NATIONALITIES

9 ..*ish*, ..*ese*, ..*ian* or something else.

Complete the table below and add some more.

Country	Nationality
Australia	Australian
Britain	British
France	French
Greece	Greek
	Russian
Holland	(a difficult one)
Italy	
	Turkish
Sudan	
Portugal	
	Spanish
Slovakia	
Denmark	
Switzerland	
Brazil	
England	
Wales	
Scotland	
Ireland	

10 Word associations Look back at your list. Choose five countries and write down three words that you link to each country.

Example Switzerland: banks, clocks, chocolate.

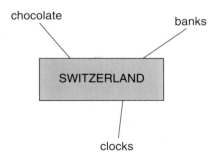

When you have finished, walk around the class and show your words. Do others agree or disagree with you?

TIME CHECK

11 Listen to this 'welcome' speech. The Principal of a language school is talking to a group of teenage students. They come from Taiwan. This is their first visit to Britain. Take notes of the important times.

12 True or false? Work in pairs and correct the statement if it is wrong.

1 The school is open all weekend. False
2 Banks are open from nine until five on weekdays. False
3 Post offices open at nine o'clock in the morning. True
4 You can get breakfast in the school at seven o'clock in the morning. True
5 Food is served all day long in the school canteen. True

13 Writing Listen to the Principal again and then, using what he says, write the information sheet for the students' welcome pack.

PRONUNCIATION

SOUNDS

❶ Read these statements. Do you agree or disagree?

- English spelling is easy because people write in the same way as they speak.
- English people speak faster in England than they do on the tapes.
- English has a lot of difficult sounds like 'th'/θ/ in *think* and 'th'/ð/ in *there* or 'ing'/ŋ/ in *listening*.
- 'Eh'/e/ and 'err'/ɜː/ are the most popular sounds in English.
- English people seem to bring their words together when they speak.

❷ Can you read aloud the alphabet in English?

A B C D E F G H I J K L M N O P Q R S T U V W X Y Z

a b c d e f g h i j k l m n o p q r s t u v w x y z

❸ Now listen to the tape. Do you have the same pronunciation? Which version do you recognise?

❹ Can you group the letters of the alphabet according to their vowel sounds? Listen to the tape for the sounds.

/eɪ/ /iː/ /e/ /aɪ/ /əʊ/ /uː/ /ɑː/ /ʌ/

❺ Now listen to the tape and check your groups.

❻ Spell your name and the address of the place where you are staying.

Note: look in the back of your book for more information about the sounds of English.

SHORT FORMS

❼ How do the phrases below sound in spoken English? How are they written?

Example I am = I'm

1 You will	6 They have	11 It is not
2 He would	7 I have not	12 We are not
3 She had	8 You did not	13 They would not
4 It is	9 He will not	14 I had not
5 We are	10 She can not	15 You could not

❽ Now listen to the tape and check your answers.

OUT OF CLASS

This is where *you* take control. Now you will direct your learning. You will go 'out of the classroom' to get your information and then you will bring it 'back into the classroom' to share with everyone.

The aims
- to collect information about shops, services and restaurants
- to compare prices and goods in Britain with prices and goods in other countries
- to practise and develop communication skills
- to work in groups
- to prepare a poster presentation

The process

❶ The class should divide into three groups.

Group A Topic: Shops
Group B Topic: Services (e.g. post offices, telephones, buses, taxis, rail etc.)
Group C Topic: Restaurants and Bars·

❷ Talk about how you can get information about your topic.

- What do you want to find out?
- What do other students want to know?
  - Think about times. Do places open/close earlier/later than in your country?
  - Think about places. How can other students get there?
  - Think about prices. Are things more or less expensive than in your country?
- How will you collect the information?
  - Will you make notes? Will you use a tape recorder?
  - Will you use places where you can get a lot of information? (Tourist information centres, libraries, museums etc.)
- Who will do this and who will do that?
  - Will your group all look for the same information?
  - Will small groups go to different places?
  - Will one person ask all the questions?
  - Will the group share the tasks?
- When will you finish?
  - Think about the time.
  - How long will you need for each task?
  - How long will you need for the whole project?
  - Work out a timetable.

- Who will manage the project?
  - Each group should have a 'manager'. S/he will decide what to do when the group have different ideas and cannot agree.

Think about:
- The names of things, (e.g. The butcher's shop: chicken, lamb, beef, etc.)
- Useful expressions and phrases:
  - Excuse me. Can you help me...
  - Hello, we're students from the....school and we're looking for information about.........................
  - We want the information to help other students in the school.
  - Can you tell us: - where the bus station is?
    - when the shop closes?
    - what time the post office opens?
    - how much the tickets cost?
    - the name of this?
    - what you call this in English?

OUTSIDE THE CLASSROOM

❸ Make sure you:

- ask the right questions.
  - Write down some of your questions to help you remember everything. Ask someone with good handwriting to make notes of your expressions for the whole group.
- collect the information.
  - Remember that people are often busy.
  - How do you begin the conversation?
  - Do you sound polite in English?
  - Repeat your question if people don't understand you.
  - Be ready for new information.
  - How do you end the conversation?
  - How do you say 'thank you' and 'goodbye'?
- pick up leaflets, brochures, tickets, receipts, cards, timetables, etc.
  - Pick up as much as you can. You can decide later what you want to use in your poster.

- think about how you are using English.
  - Remember that you will need different styles of language to speak to different people.
  - How do you ask for information from another student who is a friend?
  - How do you ask for information from someone you have never spoken to before?
  - How do you ask for information from someone in your host family?
- develop your confidence.*
  - Don't be afraid to ask questions.
  - Don't be shy. Remember, you will learn from your mistakes.
  - Say who you are and where you are from.
  - Explain clearly what you are doing and what you want.
  - Be direct and be clear.
  - Remember, people usually want to help you.

BACK INTO THE CLASSROOM

❹ • Share your experiences and show each other your information. Decide how you want to present your information on the poster.
- Prepare the poster and display it.
- Study the posters and talk about them.

- Write statements of praise for each poster. Write down any questions you want to ask. Stick these comments on the poster.

*CONFIDENCE ['kɒnfɪdəns] is about feeling good and strong about the way you speak in English.

REVIEW

WHAT KIND OF LANGUAGE LEARNER ARE YOU?

❶ Write your answers to these questions.

General

1 Why are you learning English?
   For your job? ☐
   To study? ☐
   Other reasons? ☐

2 Do any of your friends or people in your family speak English?

   _____

3 How many languages do you speak?

   _____

   Which ones?

   _____

Personal

4 Do you like travelling to foreign countries and meeting new people?

   _____

5 You are in a new country where you do not speak the language. Do you
   - try to learn a few useful phrases? ☐
   - try to find people who can speak your language? ☐
   - use your hands? ☐

6 You are at a party. Do you spend the evening talking to your friends or do you try to meet new people?

   _____

Learning

7 What are/were your best subjects at school?

   _____

8 How do you remember things better?
   If you hear them? ☐
   If you see them? ☐

9 If you have a problem, do you like to
   - get help from a teacher?
   - find the answer for yourself?

10 How do you like to work?
   Alone? ☐
   With one other person? ☐
   In a group of people? ☐

11 When do you like to work?
   Mornings? ☐
   Afternoons? ☐
   Evenings? ☐
   Late at night? ☐

Language Learning

12 Do you enjoy
   - jokes? ☐
   - stories? ☐
   - language games? ☐

13 How do you learn a foreign language?
   By studying grammar and vocabulary? ☐
   By listening and talking to people? ☐
   Both of these ways? ☐

❷ Pairwork Share your answers with a partner. Are your ways of learning the same, a little different or very different? Report to the class.

Questionnaire: British ways – What do you think about life in Britain?

❸ When we visit a foreign country for the first time, we usually have some ideas about the people and their way of life. Then, when we arrive, we notice all kinds of things. Some things are the same and some are different. Often, after some time, we get to know the country and the people a bit better and our ideas change again.

What do you and other students in your class (or in other classes in your school) think about Britain and the British way of life? In pairs, prepare 15-20 questions to find out. (There is another questionnaire activity at the end of this course to see how people's ideas change.)

Some topics to ask about:
food/eating prices houses clothes transport politeness

Some useful questions:
- What do you think of British ...[noun] ...?
- Do you think British people are ...[adjective] ...?
- What do you like/dislike about ...[noun] ... in Britain?
- Do you like British ...[noun] ...?
- Do you think ...[noun] ... in Britain is/are cheap/expensive?

UNIT REVIEW

❹ New words
How many new words can you remember from this unit? (Don't look back and don't look at your own vocabulary notes!) Make lists under different headings in the space below.

Examples
- Parts of speech (nouns, verbs, adjectives etc.)
- Topics (shopping, transport, countries etc.)
- Groups of words (shapes, colours, numbers etc.)

What other headings do you need?

❺ Writing

Describe your room (either at home or in the house you are staying in). Describe the things in the room. Write about sizes (how big/small), shapes and colours.

WHAT DO YOU SAY?

❻ How do you
- start a conversation with a stranger?
- thank someone?
- say 'sorry'?
- ask for something in a shop?
- ask the name of something?

- ask the meaning of a word?
- reply when someone says *How do you do?*
- reply when someone says *How are you?*
- say 'Hello' to someone you know very well?
- ask where someone is from?

SUPPLEMENTARY GRAMMAR PRACTICE EXERCISES

Question forms

❶ Write questions for the answers.

1   Yes, I'm studying English.
2   In Cambridge.
3   No, I'm only staying one more week.
4   I'm living with an English family.
5   From Monday to Friday.
6   We have lessons in the morning and trips in the afternoon.
7   There are twelve of us.
8   From all over the world.
9   On Wednesday afternoons.
10 Yes, I'm having a wonderful time.

❷ Use the words below to make questions.

1   How many students/your class?
2   Which countries/come from?
3   have lunch/school?
4   get a lot/homework?
5   use/English-English dictionary?

❸ Use *Wh-/How* question words to complete the following conversation.

1   _____'s the library?

    It's opposite the theatre.
2   _____ does it open?

    It opens at ten and closes at eight.
3   _____ can I join the library?

    Oh, it's very simple. You just fill in a form.
4   _____ does it cost to join?

    It's free, but you have to pay to borrow tapes, CDs and videos.
5   _____ books can you borrow?

    I think you can take six.
6   And _____ can you keep them?

    For three weeks.
7   _____ happens if you keep them for longer?

    Oh, then you do have to pay something. I think it's 10p per day for each book.

❹ Write short answers for the questions below. Add another sentence to your answer to give more information.

Example
Do you like coffee?
Yes, I do. I love it.
    or
No, I don't. I can't stand it.

1   Have you got any brothers or sisters?
2   Do your parents speak English?
3   Do you live in a city?
4   Can you drive?
5   Are your teachers all British?
6   Does your school have a language lab?
7   Are there any students from your country at the school?
8   Can your teacher speak your language?
9   Can students use the school library in the evenings?
10 Is your accommodation near the school?
11 Has your room got a desk?
12 Are you enjoying your stay in Britain?

❺ Write short questions to reply to the sentences below.

Example
It's getting late.
Is it?

1   I'm feeling hungry.
2   They're working hard.
3   There aren't any answers in the book.
4   There's a good film on TV tonight.
5   I don't understand.
6   She enjoys reading.
7   My host family are very friendly.
8   This exercise is very easy.
9   My brother is staying with me this week.
10 I've got a lot of homework this evening.

❻ Complete the sentences below with question tags.

Examples
You're a student, *aren't you?*
You're not English, *are you?*

1   He's a teacher, _____?

2   These exercises aren't difficult,

    _____?

3 She doesn't eat meat, _____?

4 The ticket isn't expensive, _____?

5 The train leaves at six-thirty, _____?

6 You come from Madrid, _____?

7 They don't drink alcohol, _____?

8 You're taking the exam today, _____?

9 The journey takes about two hours,

   _____?

10 It's too hot to work today, _____?

❼ Some of the questions below have a word missing. Write in the correct form of the verb *do* or write Ø if the question is already correct.

1 How many students _____ live in the university residences?

2 Who _____ comes from a country outside the EU?

3 How much _____ a return ticket to London cost?

4 Which books _____ you want to buy?

5 Which trains _____ stop at Colchester?

6 What music _____ you like?

7 How long _____ your lessons last?

8 Who _____ understands this question?

9 Which buses _____ leave from the station?

10 What _____ you want to eat?

❽ Use the words in the box to complete the following sentences.

when	how many	no	period	does
object	which	places	yes	do

1 Answers to questions beginning with *Where* give you information about _____.

2 If you want information about a time, you ask a question beginning with _____ or *What time*.

3 You ask questions beginning with *How long* to get information about a _____ of time.

4 You use _____ to ask about a limited number of things.

5 You begin a question with *What* when you don't know _____ answers are possible.

6 The answers to questions beginning with *Is/Are*,

Has/Have and *Does/Do* always begin with _____ or _____.

7 When a *Wh-* question word comes before the subject of the sentence, you don't need to add _____ or _____.

8 You have to add *do* or *does* when the question word is the _____ of the sentence.

❾ Correct the questions below.

✗ 1 What time your lesson finish?

2 What means *surname*?

3 What you are waiting for?

4 Do you can change a five-pound note?

5 Is ringing the phone?

6 Do you be enjoying your stay in Britain?

7 Like you Indian food?

8 Who does teach your class?

❿ Write questions to ask in the situations below.

1 To a police officer in the street.

2 To your teacher in the classroom.

3 To your host family at dinner.

4 To a bus driver on a bus.

5 To an assistant in a bank.

6 To an assistant in a shop.

⓫ Now answer these questions about yourself.

• Where do you come from?

• What do you do?

• What are you doing while you're in Britain?

• Where are you staying?

• What time do you get up in the morning?

• How do you travel to school?

• What do you do in the evenings?

• What time do you go to bed?

• Do you like English food?

• Are you enjoying your stay?

UNIT 2

24

GETTING ABOUT

In this unit you will find:

- language practice to help you
    - ask for and give the directions to get somewhere;
    - ask for things using 'got';
    - ask for help politely;
    - offer things using 'Would you like to...?';

- vocabulary to help you talk about
    - travel and transport;
    - things in the classroom;
    - days, months and years;
    - entertainments;

- pronunciation work on
    - the vowel sounds of English;
    - the 'double vowel' sounds of English;
    - the consonant sounds of English;

- your 'Out of class' project
    - to prepare a simple 'Student's Guide' for your British town;
    - to include star ratings for restaurants, cafés, clubs, etc.;
    - to write the guide for new students;

- grammar points to teach you about
    - the simple past tense;
    - regular and irregular verbs;
    - prepositions of time;
    - the past progressive tense.

SECTION 1

HOW CAN I GET TO ...?

❶ What are these things, people and places called in your language? Do you know the words in English?

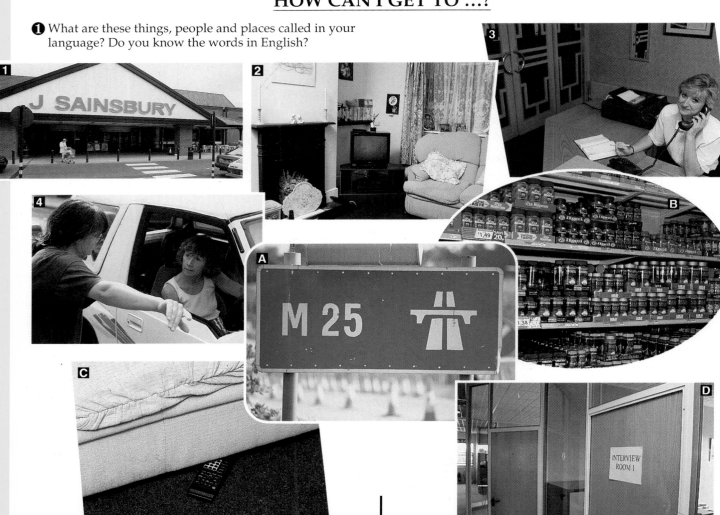

❷ Match the two groups of pictures.

❸ **Pairwork**   With a partner, take turns to ask and answer questions about the pictures.

Examples

Questions: *What/who/where is/are he/she/it/they?*
What do you think is happening?
What do you think he/she is saying?
What do you think he/she wants?
Why is .....?

Answers: *I'm not sure ...*
I think he/she wants to find ...
He/she could be a ...
He/she could be asking the way to the ...
He/she seems to be looking for ...

❹ Listen and read. Match the conversations with the pictures.

a
- Good morning, sir. Can I help you?
- Yes, I've got an appointment to see Ms Palmer.
- Ah yes, she's expecting you. You go up in the lift to the second floor, turn left and she's in the interview room at the end of the office.
- Thank you.

b
- Hello. Excuse me, can you help me? I think I'm lost.
- Yes?
- I want to get to the motorway.
- Right. Umm... well, you're on the right road. Carry on for about a mile until you reach a large roundabout and take the second turn. I think it's signposted.
- Great, thanks.

26

c

- Where's the remote control? Has anyone seen it? I can't find it anywhere.
- Have you looked under the sofa?
- Oh yes, here it is, thanks. What's it doing under the sofa?
- I don't know. You had it last.

d

- Excuse me, do you work here?
- Yes, can I help you?
- I'm after some coffee and I can't find it anywhere.
- Ah, well, all of the coffee is kept in the middle of the third aisle on the left-hand side as you go down towards the meat counter. It's there on the left, between the tea and the soft drinks.

❺ Pairwork Use the expressions below to ask your partner where you can find some of these things.

- the nearest bank
- the best café in the town
- the school staffroom
- the local museum
- the nearest toilet
- the best music shop in the town

Examples

Questions:	Answers:
Where is ...?	*It's on the ...*
I'm after ...	*You go up/down ...*
I want to get to ...	*You turn left/right at the ...*
I'm trying to find ...	*Take the ...*

❻ Listen and write the missing words. Who are the speakers? Where are they?

- Hello, can you help me? I want to go on a sightseeing _____ of Oxford. Can I get some information from you, please?
- Yes, _____. Well, there are a lot of organised tours. Would you like a bus tour _____ a walking tour?
- Oh, I would like to walk.
- Would you like a specialist tour with a full history of the Bodleian Library or a _____ tour?
- A general tour, please.
- Right, well there is a _____ tour beginning at _____ this afternoon. It starts just in front of the church of St Mary Magdalen and lasts for _____ two hours.
- That sounds good. Can you tell me a little more about it?

❼ Now listen to the man from the tourist information office. He is explaining the route of the general tour. While you listen, draw a line on the map to show the walk.

❽ Pairwork Decide where you are going to start, then take turns to ask and answer questions about how to get to places on the map.

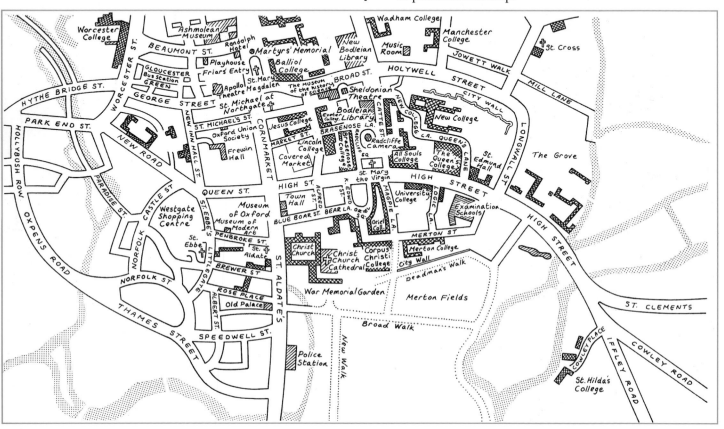

SECTION 2

HAVE YOU GOT …?

❶ Pairwork Take turns with your partner to ask each other about the photograph opposite.

- Where can you see these things?
- What are they called?
- What are they for?
- What are the connections between them?

❷ Which of these sentences is true? Look at the pictures and decide.

a
1 The student is buying a ticket.
2 The student is asking a question.
3 The clerk looks friendly.
4 The clerk is giving the student something.

b
1 The conductor wants to see the student's ticket.
2 The student can't find his ticket.
3 The conductor is angry.
4 The student does not have a ticket.

c
1 There is a big choice of food and drink.
2 The student is asking a question.
3 The steward looks unfriendly.
4 The steward is giving the student something.

❸ Now write true sentences for all of the pictures.

❹ Pairwork What do you think the student says to the clerk, the conductor and the steward? What do you think they say to him? Work in pairs and write down the conversations.

❺ Act out your conversations for the rest of the class.

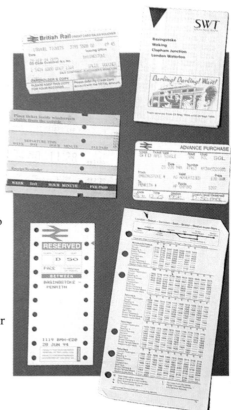

❻ Now listen to the conversations on tape and compare them with what you wrote in Exercise 4.

WHAT DO YOU THINK?

❼ Pairwork   Take turns to ask and answer the questions.

Are the trains in Britain
slower
cleaner
cheaper
more modern   than in your country?
better
more crowded
more comfortable.

Yes, they are.
No, they aren't. They're
faster/dirtier/more expensive etc.

❽ Pairwork   Work with your partner, one of you as conductor and one as passenger. Plan the conversation, but don't write it. Practise it and then act it out for the rest of the class.

Conductor	Passenger
You want to see the passenger's ticket.	You've got a ticket, but you can't find it.
You're not sure if s/he's got a ticket.	You explain the problem.
S/he hasn't got a ticket; a new one costs £20. Passengers can pay by cheque.	You've only got £10 in cash and you haven't got a cheque book.
Ask the passenger to look again.	You look again – and find your ticket.

❾ Pairwork   Take it in turns to find out about the house/room where your partner is living. Then ask about his/her host family.

Examples

Has   your room got a carpet?   Yes, it has.
      the house got a garage?   No, it hasn't, but it has
                                   got two bathrooms.

Have you got your own room?   Yes, I have.
      your family got a   No, they haven't but
      CD player?   they have got three
                                   TVs.

You can use this vocabulary to help you.

your room	*your host family*	*your accommodation*
bedside table	children	an open fire
bedside light	a car	an attic (a room in the roof)
desk	a dog	a cellar (a room below the ground)
telephone	lots of books	double glazing (double windows)

DESCRIPTIONS

❿ Listen and choose the correct pictures.

⓫ Choose the right words for the pictures.

a headache   a stomach ache   a pain in my back
a sore foot   a terrible cold

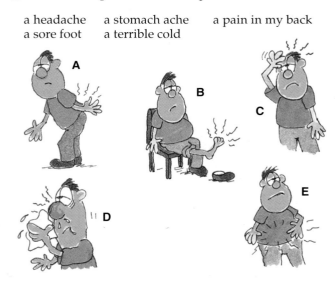

⓬ Pairwork   Describe something that you have seen in Britain. Talk about colour, size, shape and other things that you can see. Can your partner guess what it is? Don't make it too easy!

Example

They are silver, gold and brown. Two of them have got seven sides and the others are all round. They are quite small. One of them has got words on it and the others have all got words and a number. They've all got a picture of the Queen on one side.

Answer: British coins

I WONDER IF YOU COULD ...?

1 Look at the pictures. Which words would you use to describe the relationship between the people?

friends   semi-formal
strangers   informal
formal   polite

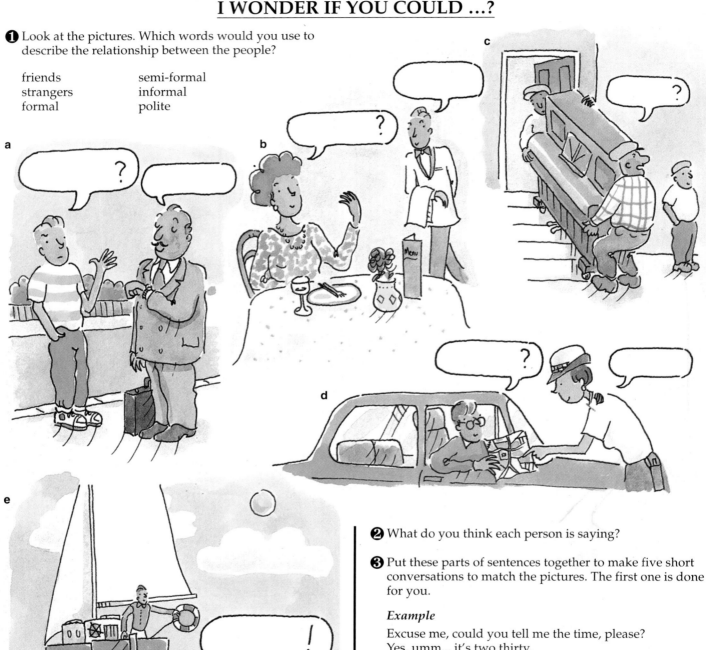

2 What do you think each person is saying?

3 Put these parts of sentences together to make five short conversations to match the pictures. The first one is done for you.

Example

Excuse me, could you tell me the time, please?
Yes, umm... it's two thirty.

Certainly, sir.
could you tell me the time, please?
Could I have the bill, please?
Could you tell me how I can get to the station?
Excuse me,
Give us a hand, can you?
I'll bring it straight away.
it's two thirty.
Sure.
Yes of course, Madam,
Yes, umm...
Help!

❹ Now listen to the tape and compare the conversations with what you have written.

❺ How *can I* get to the station?/Could you tell me *how I can* get to the station?

Use the prompts to make questions like those above. Be careful with word order and punctuation.

1 How/get/to the airport
2 Could/tell/how/get/to the airport
3 How/make/telephone call to Ankara
4 Could /tell/how/make/telephone call to Ankara
5 When/does/train/leave
6 Could/tell/when/train/leave
7 How much/this watch/cost
8 Could/tell/how much/this watch/cost
9 What/time/be/it
10 Could/tell/what/time/be

POLITE AND VERY POLITE

❻ Some people say that the English are 'cold'. Some people say that the English are 'formal'. Some people say that the English are 'shy'. What do you think?

Look at the following expressions. Who do you think is speaking? Who do you think they are speaking to? Where do you think they are?

- Give me a glass of water.
- I wonder if I could possibly trouble you for a glass of water?

- I wonder if you could possibly give me a glass of water?
- Please could you give me a glass of water.
- I wonder if you could give me a glass of water, please?
- I wonder if you could give me a glass of water?
- Could you give me a glass of water?
- Can you give me a glass of water?
- I want a glass of water.

❼ Now listen to the expressions and repeat them using the same intonation.

❽ Listen again and answer in a way that you think is right for the situation. Think about:

- where you could be;
- who you could be speaking to;
- how well you know the other person.

❾ **Pairwork**   Look at the pictures below. Who are the people? Where are they? What are they talking about? How do they speak? How formal/informal/polite/casual/relaxed/shy/rude/British are they?

❿ Write something about each picture and read it out to the rest of the class.

SECTION 4

WOULD YOU LIKE TO ...?

❶ Look at the pictures and write down all the words you think of.

❷ **Pairwork** Work in pairs and compare your lists.

❸ Ask each other:

- What can you see in the pictures?
- What do people do there?

❹ Listen to the conversations and make notes in the boxes below.

Who are the speakers?
A
B
C
D

Where are they?
A
B
C
D

What are the questions?
A
B
C
D

Other key words/phrases
A
B
C
D

❺ How would you say these expressions? Which sound more formal and which sound more relaxed? Who do you think is speaking? Who do you think they are speaking to? Where do you think they are?

1 Do you want to dance?
2 Fancy a drink?
3 Would you like to go to the cinema this evening?
4 How about going for a walk?
5 I was wondering if you'd like to come over for dinner one evening.
6 Want a cigarette?
7 Would you like to accompany me to the police station, sir?
8 Do you feel like going out this evening?

32

6 Now listen to the tape and say the expressions again.

WRITING

7 Pairwork   Choose one of the situations below and write a short conversation. When you have finished, practise it then act it out for the rest of the class.

A Two students are at home on a rainy Sunday afternoon. They have finished their homework. They have different ideas about things to do (watch TV, play cards, prepare a meal, etc.), but in the end they agree.

B Two friends are planning a weekend trip (to London, Cambridge, Stratford etc.). One of them has a guidebook and s/he has all the ideas about places to visit/things to do.

C Two students are at home on Saturday afternoon. They are talking about where to go and what to do in the evening. They have different ideas and they cannot agree.

8 Pairwork   Take turns to ask and answer questions about the pictures.

Example (Pictures A and C)

Would you like to go shopping?	Yes, I would. No, I wouldn't. I'd like to go to the cinema.

9 Pairwork   How do you spend your free time at home? What do you enjoy doing in the evenings and at weekends? Can you do the same things while you are staying in Britain? Ask each other, and then write about what your partner likes to do.

Examples

- At home he enjoys skiing and playing football, but of course he can't go skiing here. So he only plays football.
- She plays the piano, but her host family hasn't got a piano. So, while she's here she only listens to music.
- She likes Indonesian food, but there aren't any Indonesian restaurants here. So she goes to a Chinese restaurant.

Unit 2

GRAMMAR

LANGUAGE PRACTICE

TALKING ABOUT PAST TIME

Talking about the past

❶ Think about yesterday and complete the passage below. What do the underlined words show you?

Yesterday I <u>got</u> up at _____ and <u>had</u> my breakfast <u>at</u> _____. Breakfast <u>took about</u> _____ minutes. I <u>left</u> home at _____ and <u>went</u> to _____. <u>During</u> the morning I _____ and <u>then</u> I <u>had</u> lunch at _____. <u>In the afternoon</u> I _____ and then I <u>went</u> home <u>at</u> _____. My supper <u>lasted</u> <u>from</u> _____ to _____ and <u>then</u> I _____. I _____ to bed <u>at</u> _____ and slept <u>from</u> _____ <u>to</u> _____.

Irregular verbs

❷ Correct the verbs in the sentences below.

1 He getted up at seven.
2 She goed to the cinema.
3 I seed him in the bookshop.
4 She comed by bus.
5 Where you have lunch yesterday?
6 I missed the bus and so I taked a taxi to the cinema.
7 I thinked the film was really good.
8 She feeled sick yesterday and so she goed to the doctor.

What was happening?

❸ Look at the pictures and write down what the man was doing.

❹ **Pairwork**   With your partner, spend a few minutes thinking about the conversation between the man and his wife. How does he explain himself? Then act out the situation for the rest of the class.

❺ Can you explain the differences between the pairs of sentences below? Use the time-lines on the next page to help you.

1 He was watching television when his wife came home.
   He watched television when his wife came home.
2 He went to the shops when it started to snow.
   He was going to the shops when it started to snow.
3 The band was playing when the bomb exploded.
   The band played when the bomb exploded.

❻ Write answers for these questions to tell your life story. Write full sentences.

1 When were you born?
2 Where were you brought up?
3 Where did you go to school?
4 How long did your school day last?
5 What did you do in the evenings after school?
6 When did you leave school?
7 Then what did you do?

NOTE - to do the washing up = to wash the plates, cutlery etc. after a meal.

34

LANGUAGE STUDY

GRAMMAR POINTS 1

A Moments in time and periods of time in the past. The simple past and prepositions of time.

- You can use the simple past to talk about (a) a fixed moment in the past or (b) a period of time in the past.

Examples
a I went out *at* eight o'clock.
b I lived in London *for* three years.

```
                    8 o'clock
                        X          •
    PAST                          NOW

             3 years
    X X X X X X X              •
         PAST                  NOW
```

- You can use key words (prepositions of time) to show whether you are talking about a fixed moment or a longer period.

Fixed moment	*Longer period*
at (times, e.g. eight o'clock)	for (any period of time, e.g. two seconds or 200 years
on (days of the week, e.g. Monday)	in/during (e.g. January; years, e.g. 1995)

```
    X  X  X  X  X  X  X  X   •
             PAST            NOW

                     I phoned
                        ↓
    X   X   X   X   X   X   X  • X   X        •
             PAST                          NOW
```

- Most regular verbs form the simple past by adding *-ed* or *-d* or *-t*. However, many common verbs are 'irregular' and you must learn a different form for the simple past tense. There is no short cut to this!

Examples

go	went	drink	drank
have	had	take	took
be	was	come	came
feel	felt	make	made
get	got	give	gave
see	saw	think	thought

GRAMMAR POINTS 2

- Negative forms of the simple past tense are made using *didn't* (did not) and the infinitive of the verb.

Examples
She *didn't come home* last night.
He *didn't like* school.

- Question forms in the simple past tense are made using *did* or *didn't* and the infinitive of the verb.

Examples
What time *did* you *get up* yesterday?
Did you *see* the film last night?
Where *did* you *have lunch*?

- Negative and question forms of the verb 'to be' in the simple past are an exception. They are made using *was/wasn't*.

Examples
Was the train late?   *not*   Did the train be late?
No, the train wasn't late.   No, it didn't be late.

GRAMMAR POINTS 3

B Continuing periods of activity in the past. The past progressive tense.

- You can use the past progressive to describe things that were happening over a period of time at a specific point in the past.

The past progressive is formed using the simple past tense of the verb 'to be' and the *-ing* form of the main verb.

Examples
I *was working* in the garden all morning.
S/he *was watching* television.
You *were listening* to the radio.
We *were enjoying* the meal.
You *were talking* together.
They *were playing* football.

GRAMMAR POINTS 4

The past progressive often combines with the simple past, using *when* or *while*.

Example
I *was doing* my homework *when* the phone rang.
While I *was swimming*, someone stole my clothes.

GRAMMAR POINTS 5

- Negative forms in the past progressive tense are made using *wasn't* or *weren't* and the *-ing* form of the main verb.

Examples
I *wasn't doing* anything special.
You *weren't waiting* outside the cinema.
S/he *wasn't expecting* a phone call yesterday.
We *weren't running away*.
You *weren't following* us.
They *weren't riding* their bicycles.

- Question forms in the past progressive tense are made using *was/wasn't* or *were/weren't* and the *-ing* form of the main verb.

Examples
Was I *disturbing* you?
Weren't you *driving* to York last Monday?
Was s/he *behaving* badly?
Were(n't) we/you/they *having dinner* at seven o'clock?

VOCABULARY

A TRANSPORT

❶ Which of these things can you find in the picture?

bicycle bus pedestrian car taxi van lorry

❷ Which word/phrase does not belong in each of the following lists? Why not? Use a dictionary to help you.

1 passenger conductor ticket customer station platform
2 bonnet boot steering wheel gears brakes tyres remote control
3 boarding card dock immigration gate customs departure lounge
4 minibus coach compartment taxi motorcycle ferry minicab
5 road rail air sea street underground foot

B IN THE CLASSROOM

❸ How many of the things in the list below can you see in your classroom? Where are they? Use these words (prepositions) to describe where they are.

in on next to near between opposite above
below behind in front of

- cassette player
- video (VCR)
- television (TV)
- overhead projector (OHP)
- blackboard
- whiteboard
- notice board
- clothes hooks
- wastepaper bin
- bookcase
- shelves
- posters
- screen
- map
- chalk
- clock

C POLITE EXPRESSIONS

❹ Choose the right expression for each of the situations below. (In some situations it may be possible to use more than one of them.)

- Thanks
- I'm sorry to bother you. ·
- Don't mention it.
- I'd love to.
- I'm terribly sorry. ·
- Thank you very much.
- That's very kind of you.
- It's nothing.
- That's just what I wanted.
- Don't worry about it. ·
- Excuse me. ·
- Not at all.
- Yes, please.

1 Your host family are watching television. You want to ask them for some information. What do you say?

2 You are on a crowded bus. You arrive at your stop and as you get up, you drop your school books on to an old woman's foot. What do you say?

3 Your host family invite you to a special family dinner. You don't understand that the dinner is for your landlady's birthday. The other guests all bring presents and you tell her you are very sorry that you haven't got a present for her. What does she say?

4 You are travelling by train with a friend. You are carrying two cups of coffee back to your compartment and another passenger opens a connecting door for you. What do you say?

5 A friend gives you a lift home from a party. You know that he lives on the other side of town and you thank him. What does he say?

6 You are having tea with your host family. Your landlady offers you a second piece of her home-made cake. What do you say?

8 You are travelling home by plane with a friend, but you find that your seats are not together. Another passenger offers to change places with you and you thank her. What does she say?

9 You leave your gloves in a restaurant. The waiter runs after you and gives you the gloves. What do you say?

10 You are in a department store. You want some information, but the assistant is talking to a colleague. What do you say?

11 You are in a tourist information office. You want some information about trips to Scotland. The assistant gives you a lot of brochures and leaflets and you thank her. What does she say?

12 It is Sunday afternoon and you are feeling very bored. Your host family invite you to go for a drive in the countryside. What do you say?

13 A friend has two free tickets for a concert. She knows that you like classical music and she offers you the tickets. What do you say?

36

5 Say the expressions in Exercise 4. Then listen to them on tape.

D DAYS, MONTHS AND YEARS

6 Find the days of the week and put them into the right order.

ODMAYN   NEDDYWESA   ARDYUTAS   RAFDIY
YADSUET   DUNSAY   RUDYTHAS

7 Can you say the names of the days? Listen to the tape and check your pronunciation.

8 Write the full names of the months of the year and put them into the right order.

- Feb • Apr • Jul • Oct • Mar • Aug
- May • Dec • Sept • Jun • Nov • Jan

9 How do you say the names of the months in English? Are they similar in your language or are they very different? Listen and check your pronunciation.

E NUMBERS

10 Complete this list of numbers.

1 one	1st _____ *	11 _____	11th _____ *
2 _____	2nd second*	12 twelve	12th _____ *
3 three	3rd _____ *	13 _____	13th _____ *
4 _____	4th _____ *	14 _____	14th _____ *
5 five	5th _____ *	15 _____	15th fifteenth*
6 six	6th _____ *	16 _____	16th _____ *
7 _____	7th _____ *	17 _____	17th _____ *
8 eight	8th _____ *	18 _____	18th _____ *
9 nine	9th _____ *	19 nineteen	19th _____ *
10 _____	10th _____ *	20 twenty	20th _____ *

11 Say the numbers marked with a [*]. Then listen and check your pronunciation.

F DATES

12 You can write the date in different ways, but there is only one way to say it.

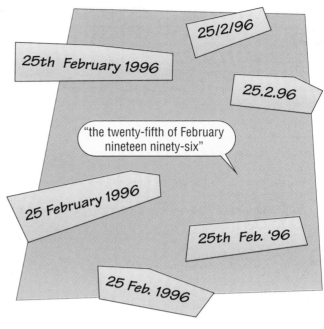

25/2/96

25th February 1996

25.2.96

"the twenty-fifth of February nineteen ninety-six"

25 February 1996

25th Feb. '96

25 Feb. 1996

13 Say the following dates. Then listen to them on the tape.

1 2 Sept '95   4 18 April 1975
2 8/8/88   5 1.1.91
3 3rd December 1968   6 11th Nov 1999

G ENTERTAINMENTS

14 Find the right words or phrases from the box to complete sentences 1 – 10 below.

cinema	on the door	in advance	performance
nightclub	front row	films stalls	theatre
plays	box office	concert	

1 Tickets are £6.50 .... or £8 ....
2 The town is very quiet after 11 p.m., but there's a .... which is open until two in the morning.
3 The local .... has an 'open' stage – the audience sit on three sides of the actors.
4 It was a fantastic .... The orchestra played some of my favourite music.
5 I used to enjoy acting in .... when I was at school.
6 I don't like sitting in the .... at the .... It's too close to the screen.
7 We queued for half an hour at the .... to book our tickets.
8 I like sitting downstairs in the .... but those seats are usually more expensive.
9 When I watch .... on video, I can rewind the tape and listen again if I don't understand.
10 There is one .... every evening from Monday to Saturday, with a matinee on Wednesday afternoon.

Unit 2

37

PRONUNCIATION

SOUNDS

VOWELS

The diagram below shows the positions of the 12 basic vowel sounds of English. The weak form schwa /ə/ (as in *performance* /pəˈfɔːməns/) is the most common vowel sound in English, and is present in almost all languages.

The left-hand side of the diagram shows the sounds at the front of the mouth.
The right-hand side shows the sounds at the back of the mouth.
You make the sounds at the top of the diagram with your lips quite close together.
You make the sounds at the bottom with your mouth more open.

❶ You practised the vowels shown in the diagram in Unit 1. Can you find the right places for the other vowel sounds? Listen to these examples.

/æ/	as in m<u>a</u>gazine	/mægəˈziːn/
/ɒ/	.. .. c<u>o</u>ncert	/ˈkɒnsət/
/ɔː/	.. .. sp<u>o</u>rt	/ˈspɔːt/
/ʊ/	.. .. f<u>oo</u>tball	/ˈfʊtbɔːl/
/ɪ/	.. .. c<u>i</u>nema	/ˈsɪnəmə/

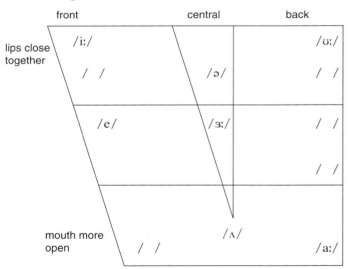

front	central	back
lips close together /iː/		/uː/
/ /	/ə/	/ /
/e/	/ɜː/	/ /
		/ /
mouth more open / /	/ʌ/	/aː/

❷ The vowel sound in 'house' is a **double** sound. You make it by putting two of the 12 basic sounds together:
/aː/ + /ʊ/ = /aʊ/

Which of the following vowels go together to make the double sounds underlined in the words below?
/ə/ /ɪ/ /e/ /a/ /ɒ/ /ʊ/

1 pr<u>i</u>ce
2 t<u>ou</u>r
3 app<u>oi</u>ntment
4 s<u>a</u>le

5 ph<u>o</u>ne
6 squ<u>are</u>
7 th<u>ea</u>tre

❸ Listen to the tape to check your pronunciation.

CONNECTIONS

You make vowel sounds by changing the shape of your mouth and keeping your lips open.

All the sounds which are *not* vowels are called **consonants**. To make consonant sounds, you use your lips, tongue, teeth and the roof of your mouth.

When a word ends with a consonant sound and the next word begins with a vowel, the two words are pronounced like a single word.

Example
this afternoon

a cup of tea

❹ Draw lines in the same way to show the sound connections in the following sentences.

1 He's got brown eyes and a long, thin face.
2 I've got a terrible pain in my back.
3 I've been on my feet all day.
4 I'd like some information about air fares, please.
5 Don't worry about it.
6 Would you like a cup of coffee?
7 I was born on the first of April, nineteen fifty-eight.
8 The town is very quiet after about eleven o'clock.
9 Have you got an appointment?
10 Carry on for about a mile.

❺ Now check your answers against the tape.

38

OUT OF CLASS

Remember that this is where *you* are in control. You decide what you are going to do and how to do it. You will go 'out of the classroom' again to collect your information. When you come 'back into the classroom', you will put all the information together to make a basic guide to the town for new students.

The aims

- to prepare a simple, basic Student's Guide to the town where you are studying.
- to collect important facts and figures (times, prices, directions) for new students arriving in the town
- to practise communicating in English
- to work in groups

The process

❶ The class should divide into four groups.

Group A — Topic: Sport and Entertainment (e.g. tennis courts, cinemas, theatres, nightclubs etc.)

Group B — Topic: Food and Drink

Group C — Topic: Shops and Services (e.g. banks, post offices, tourist information etc.)

Group D — Topic: Sightseeing

❷ Talk about how you can get information about your topic.

- What are the most important things for new students to know?
  - Which places are the cheapest? Which are the most expensive?
  - Are there any places which are cheaper for students?
  - Which places close early? Which stay open late?
  - Which places are the best? Which ones do students usually like?

- Where can you get the information you need?
  - Can you get any information from the local paper? or on the telephone?
  - Who can you ask? Your host family? teachers? other students?
- How will you divide the work in your group?
  - Will you look for information about things you like? Or will you look for information about new things?
- How much time will you need?
  - Remember to work out a timetable. Give yourselves enough time to do everything. You will probably find it helpful to divide your group into pairs.
- Who will be the group 'manager'?
  - Is there anyone in your group who managed the 'out of class' work in Unit 1? Does s/he want to do it again? Does anyone else want to do it?

Think about:

- landmarks (things like statues, churches or other large buildings)
  - How can people find places easily?
- transport
  - How can people get to places?

Look back at the expressions and phrases in Unit 1. Here are some more. Can you think of any others?

Have you got any information about _____?
Are there any reductions for students?
How often do you change your programme?
Have you got any leaflets about _____?
Do you need a membership card?
Can you buy tickets on the door? Or do you have to book in advance?
Can you pay by cheque? Do you accept credit cards?

OUTSIDE THE CLASSROOM

❸ Make sure you:

- explain what you are doing – and why
  - Say who you are and where you come from. If people are not too busy, they will usually be helpful.
- prepare your questions carefully
  - Make notes of all the things you want to know.

- collect – or record – the information
  - In some places you can take away leaflets, brochures, timetables. etc. If there aren't any, be prepared to make notes or (if you have the facilities) audio/video recordings.
- think about how you are using your English
  - Remember to be polite – especially to people that you don't know.

BACK IN THE CLASSROOM

❹
- Share your information with the other groups.
- Decide how you are going to put the information together to make the Student's Guide. The Guide could be a photocopied leaflet or a wall display. It should include a map of the town centre and give important information for new students (e.g. times, prices etc.).
- Think about how to show the quality of different places. For example, you could use a simple star (★) system: ★★★★ = excellent, ★★★ = very good, ★★ = quite good, ★ = not very good.

- Decide how you are going to produce the Guide. Will different groups write their own pages and then put them together? Or will you form new groups to share the information and produce different guides?
- Think about other information that you can add to the Guide. For example, you could use a display of photographs, audio recordings (interviews, telephone messages) or a short video film.
- Prepare a short questionnaire to find out what other students think about the Guide. Ask for ideas about how you could improve it.

Unit 2

HOW IS YOUR VISIT TO BRITAIN HELPING YOUR ENGLISH?

WHAT ARE YOU LEARNING ABOUT BRITAIN?

❶ Tick the boxes that describe your habits.

	sometimes	often	never
I watch the television.	☐	☐	☐
I listen to the radio.	☐	☐	☐
I spend a lot of time talking to British people.	☐	☐	☐
I spend a lot of time speaking in my own language.	☐	☐	☐
I listen to strangers talking.	☐	☐	☐
I read English newspapers and magazines.	☐	☐	☐
I look carefully at posters and advertisements.	☐	☐	☐
I read the names of the shops and study the notices in the windows.	☐	☐	☐
I write down the words of the English songs that I listen to.	☐	☐	☐
I ask people to help me when I don't know how to say something.	☐	☐	☐
I go to the cinema.	☐	☐	☐
I go to the theatre.	☐	☐	☐
I use the town library and the information centre.	☐	☐	☐
I use the school language laboratory.	☐	☐	☐

❷ **Pairwork** Compare your answers with a partner. What advice can you give to each other?

❸ How helpful do you find these activities? With your partner, give each activity a star rating (five stars ★★★★★ for the most useful).

❹ Compare your ratings with another pair, then decide which activities tell you most about life in Britain. Number them in order from most (1) to least (15) informative.

WRITING

❺ Complete the sentences below.

1 Before I came to Britain I thought the people were

_____.

2 I think the English language is _____.

3 I have discovered that _____.

4 I want to find out more about _____.

5 I don't like _____.

UNIT REVIEW

❻ Write two sentences to show the difference in meaning between the simple past and the past progressive tenses. Illustrate them with time lines.

NEW WORDS

❼ Look back over the unit and write down the words which you don't remember very well. Write down a definition for each word and then write down other words that you link to it.

Example

New word: appointment
Definition: an agreement to be with someone at a particular time and in a particular place
Link words:

meeting   interview
time —— appointment
doctor   dentist   arrangement

❽ How well are you learning? How well can you manage in English? Put a tick (✔) or a cross (✘) beside each of the statements below.

	Yes	No
I can ask for the time.	☐	☐
I can tell someone the time.	☐	☐
I can ask for directions.	☐	☐
I can give someone directions.	☐	☐
I can understand a menu and order a meal.	☐	☐
I can ask how much something costs.	☐	☐
I can deal with money in shops.	☐	☐
I can ask for information.	☐	☐
I can offer something (e.g. a drink) to someone else.	☐	☐
I can ask what a word means.	☐	☐
I can ask for help with English.	☐	☐
I can introduce myself to others.	☐	☐
I can spell out words.	☐	☐
I can find out about other people.	☐	☐
I can talk about myself and where I come from.	☐	☐

Unit 2

41

SUPPLEMENTARY GRAMMAR PRACTICE EXERCISES

❶ Rewrite these sentences with the verbs in the simple past tense.

1 I live in London.
2 I cycle three miles to school.
3 My mother signs all the cheques.
4 He looks at the photograph and cries.
5 My secretary types all my letters.
6 I work for Sony.
7 They play football on Saturdays.
8 We never learn any grammar.
9 They play well together.
10 She wants to go out with him.

❷ Complete these sentences with the correct prepositions of time.

1 The film began ___*at*___ eight o'clock.
2 My parents were hippies. They grew up _____ the 1960s.
3 I arrived at school a few minutes _____ 9 o'clock.
4 At my old school, the lessons lasted _____ 9.30 _____ 3.30 every day.
5 I lived in India _____ two years.
6 I left the restaurant _____ 10.30 and got home _____ 11.00.
7 We went to Oxford _____ the day _____ Monday.
8 I finished my grammar homework _____ the coffee break this morning.
9 I left school _____ eighteen, then I went to live in Italy _____ a year.
10 They reached London _____ less than an hour.

❸ Rewrite these sentences in the negative form.

1 I enjoyed the film.
2 She wanted to go to Spain.
3 They really liked the meal.
4 You went to the shops on Saturday.
5 We worked hard yesterday.

6 She practised the simple past and past progressive tenses.
7 He got a bicycle for Christmas.
8 We took the train home.
9 They offered to lend us their football.
10 He felt cold in the mountains.

❹ Use the prompts to make questions.

1 you/go/theatre/last Saturday
2 what/you/do/in Brighton
3 why/English/like/tea
4 Peter/telephone/his parents/last night
5 who/stay with/in Cambridge
6 why/choose/that restaurant
7 you/have/one or two meals/on the train
8 be/your bus/late
9 be/Maria and Eduardo/in school/yesterday
10 when/you/learn/to drive

❺ Now write answers for each of the questions in Exercise 4, using the simple past tense.

❻ Put the verbs in brackets into either the simple past or the past progressive tense.

1 I (arrive) at eight o'clock and she (have) her supper.
2 He (feed) the cat when the roof (fall) in.
3 He (step) on a banana skin while he (cross) the road. He (fall) down and a car (run) him over.
4 She (enjoy) a long, hot bath after work when the telephone (ring).
5 He (say) he (clean) his gun when it accidentally (go) off.
6 It (kill) his wife, who (watch) TV.
7 We (think about) Peter when the telephone (ring).
8 It (be) Peter, he (phone) from Brazil.
9 You (live) in Berlin when the Wall came down?
10 No, I (not live) there at the time, but Wilhelm (be).

42

❼ A policewoman is questioning someone about a crime. Write down the questions she asks for the answers below.

- _____?

- I was having a meal in 'The Golden Moon Chinese Restaurant.

- _____?

- I had Peking Duck, followed by banana fritters.

- _____?

- I left the restaurant at about nine o'clock.

- _____?

- Then I went home.

- _____?

- I walked.

- _____?

- No, I didn't notice anything strange but someone was screaming in the park.

- _____?

- Yes, they were screaming very loudly.

❽ Use your own ideas to continue the dialogue. What was happening in the park? What happened next?

❾ Use the correct form of the following verbs to complete the paragraph below.

> fly get get learn leave leave lie read
> send stay work write

I _____ university at the age of 24 and _____ a

job as a trainee reporter. After several years,

while I _____ how to be a journalist, the news editor

_____ me to West Africa. I _____ in Africa

during the civil war in Biafra. I _____ a lot in Biafra,

but after six months I _____ very ill.

I _____ home to England and _____ in hospital

for two months. I _____ a lot while I _____ in

my hospital bed. After I _____ hospital, I …

❿ Using the simple past or the past progressive tense forms, write three questions you would like to ask the journalist. Use

Why _____

_____

_____

_____?

When _____

_____

_____

_____?

What _____

_____

_____

_____?

Which _____

_____

_____

_____?

Where _____

_____

_____

_____?

How _____

_____

_____?

⓫ Correct the sentences and questions below.

1 Did the train be on time?
2 We was watching television yesterday evening.
3 I not be following you. We are living in the same street.
4 She not be expecting a phone call yesterday.
5 He liked not school.
6 How long you be waiting for me?
7 Did you be at the party last night?
8 Why you no tell me to learn the grammar?
9 You were watch television all evening, were you?
10 I come to Edinburgh for the Festival, two years ago.

Unit 2

43

Well, I think we must be going.

No, no. Do stay and have another drink

MEETING PEOPLE

In this unit you will find:

- language practice to help you
  - ask what someone does;
  - ask how long someone has been doing something;
  - ask what you say in different situations;
  - ask whose something is;

- vocabulary to help you talk about
  - clothes;
  - members of the family;
  - people, places, organisations and things using abbreviations;

- more pronunciation work on
  - vowel sounds and 'double vowel' sounds;
  - consonant sounds;

- your 'Out of class' project
  - to prepare a questionnaire;
  - to find out more about habits, customs and beliefs in Britain;
  - to present and discuss the information;

- grammar points to teach you about
  - talking about the present and the past;
  - the present simple tense;
  - the present progressive tense;
  - adverbs of frequency;
  - the present perfect tense;
  - the present perfect progressive tense.

SECTION 1

WHAT DO YOU DO?

❶ What are these things, people and places called in your language? Do you know the words in English?

❷ Match the two groups of pictures.

❸ Pairwork   Talk about the pictures, like this:

Examples

Questions:

		is s/he?		is s/he	
Where			*What*		*doing?*
		are they?		*are they*	

Where is it?   *What can you buy/find there?*

What is his/her/their job called?

Answers: *I'm not sure. I think …*
She/he/it is/could be a …
They are/could be …
She/he seems to be …
It's a place where …

❹ Listen and read. Match the conversations with the pictures.

a • Excuse me. How many books can I take out?
• You can take up to six.
• And when do I have to bring them back?
• You can keep them out for up to three weeks. If you want to keep them any longer than that, you can renew them by phone. If you don't renew them, there is a fine on all overdue books of 5p per day per book.

b • Good evening. Can I help you, sir?
  • Yes. I made a reservation last week. The name is Rodriguez.
  • Yes, here we are. Mr and Mrs Rodriguez. And you're staying for three nights. Is that correct?
  • Yes, that's right. Do you need to see our passports?
  • No, but can you fill in this registration form, please? You're in room 236 on the second floor. I'll ask the porter to take your bags up.

c • Can you write the amount in words here and in figures here?
  • Do you want to see any identification?
  • Yes, I'll need your passport. And can you write your card number on the back of the cheque, please?
  • There you are.
  • Thank you. And how would you like it?
  • Oh, three tens and four fives, please.

d • Well, there's a flight at 10.30 a.m. on the 26th from Heathrow, arriving in Rome at 12 o'clock local time. How would that suit you?
  • It's rather early. I'd have to spend the night in a hotel. Is there anything around lunchtime?
  • No, I'm afraid the later flight is fully booked. I could get you a standby ticket, but of course you wouldn't be sure of getting a seat.
  • I'd better take the earlier one, then.

❺ **Pairwork** Look at the pictures on the opposite page and find other pictures in the book of people at work. Using the questions below, ask your partner about the people in the pictures and ask about their jobs.

  • *What is s/he doing?*
  • *What does s/he do?*
  • *What do ....s do?*

Example
  • *What is s/he doing?*   *S/he's talking to the passengers on the coach.*

  • *What does s/he do?*   *S/he's a tour guide.*
  • *What do tour guides do?*   *They look after tourists.*

🔲

❻ Listen and write the missing words. Who are the speakers? Where do they work?

a 'I love _____ here. Of course I _____ the same thing every day, but it's never _____. Tourists come here from all over the world and so I meet some really _____ people. They usually _____ to the office when they first _____ and I give them a map and some information about the city. They _____ all kinds of questions and if I _____ know the answers, I always know where to look. I don't like it in the _____ when it's too quiet. I like to be _____.'

b 'The job is all right. I do all the work _____ the house. My _____ both have _____ – _____ jobs and so they need someone to look _____ the children and keep the house _____. I do the cleaning, the _____, the ironing and _____ I do the cooking, too. And then, of course, there are the children. I _____ with them and _____ them out in the afternoons. I enjoy _____ after the children most of all. But it's hard work and I really _____ got time to feel _____.'

c 'I like _____ and I _____ talking to people. So this is the _____ job for me. When I get up in the morning, I never _____ where I'm going to go that day or who I'm going to meet. Usually it's just a short _____, but _____ somebody wants to go to the airport or to the _____. It's quite _____ at the beginning, because you have to know every _____ in the city and all the routes to get from one place to _____. The worst thing is the hours, for anyone with a _____. I'm not married – so it's all right for me.'

❼ *a* You are going to hear a woman answering questions about her job. Make notes of the most important words/phrases.
  b What questions do you think the interviewer asked? Listen again and write the questions. Then compare your questions with a partner.

❽ How would you answer the interviewer's questions in the last exercise? Write your own answers. (If you are still a student, write the answers for a friend or a member of your family.)

❾ **Pairwork** Now use the questions and answers to interview each other.

SECTION 2

HOW LONG HAVE YOU ...?

❶ Work in pairs and ask each other how long you have been/are:

- learning English.
- in England.
- going to stay in England.

❷ Look at the picture stories below. Who are the people? Where are they? What is happening? Can you tell the rest of the class?

Simon and Elizabeth King,
c/o The Beach Hut Palace,
Pitcairn Island *
The South Pacific Ocean.

*Pitcairn is a small island in the middle of the Pacific Ocean. About 65 people live there. A group of English sailors ran away with women from Tahiti to live there in 1790. The film *Mutiny on the Bounty* tells their story.

❸ Is the sentence true or false, probably true or probably false? Look at the pictures and decide.

A 1 The woman is late for the lunch.
2 The man has forgotten about the appointment.
3 The woman is worried.
4 The man apologises.

B 1 The man wants to send a fax.
2 The post office clerk often sends letters to Pitcairn Island.
3 The man has relatives who live on Pitcairn.
4 The letter is not the best way of communicating with people so far away.

❹ Write new sentences to make them all true or probably true.

❺ What do you think the man and the woman say to each other? What do you think the man and the post office clerk say to each other? Work in pairs and write the conversations.

❻ Act out your conversations for the rest of the class.

❼ Read the scripts below and think about the missing words.

🔲

❽ Listen to the recordings and write down the words you hear in the blank spaces.

A Man: Hello, Darling.
  Woman: Where _____ _____ _____
            _____ _____? I've -
  Man: Look, I'm really sorry, have you been
            _____ _____ ?
  Woman: Have I been waiting long? You said
            '_____ o'clock'. You said 'Don't be
            late'. Well, what time do _____
            _____ _____ _____ _____?
            Hey?

B Man: Hello, um, I'd like _____ _____
            _____ _____ to Pitcairn please.
            Will it _____ _____ ?
  Clerk: Where did you say?
  Man: Pitcairn. It's a small island in the middle of
            the Pacific. My grandchildren are on their
            way there.
  Clerk: Oh, I see. Well it might _____
            _____ _____ _____. Have you
            thought about sending a _____ or
            even a telemessage? It will get there much
            _____ .

❾ Work in pairs. Choose one of the situations then choose one of the characters. Plan the conversation but don't write it out in full. Try it, then act it out.

Situation A

First character	*Second character*
You are waiting at the restaurant	You have arrived late
You have been waiting for forty minutes	You had forgotten about the meeting
You have been very worried about your friend	You feel embarrassed
You get angry with her/him	You say that you are sorry
You decide to order the food	

Situation B

A customer	*A clerk at the post office*
You want to send a letter home	You serve the customer
You want to know how much it will cost and how long it will take	
You explain that the letter is urgent	You recommend using a fax
You don't know anything about faxes	You explain how a fax works

❿ **Pairwork**   Punctuality and forms of apology. Ask each other about the customs in your country.

🔲

⓫ Listen to these people apologising.

Decide:
Is the relationship formal or informal?
Do the people know each other?
Where might they be (are they alone or in public)?
What has happened?

WHAT DO YOU THINK?

⓬ Read these statements and decide. Compare Britain with your own country.

The British are always saying that they are sorry.
Saying *sorry* and *excuse me* are just common expressions.
It is very difficult to apologise in any language.
There are lots of ways of saying sorry but people don't mean it.
'Love means never having to say that you are sorry.'

⓭ Talk to your partner about being late.

Have you ever arrived late:
- at a lesson?
- for a meeting?
- for dinner at a friend's house?
- for a plane or a train?

What did you say?
What reasons did you give?

Unit 3

SECTION 3

WHAT DO YOU SAY?

❶ Dinner at 8.15. Some English friends invite you to their house for dinner. What do you do? Discuss the questions with other students in your class.

1 The invitation is for 8.15. What time do you arrive?
2 Do you take anything (e.g. a present) for your friends? If so, what do you take?
3 The food is delicious. Do you ask for more?
4 Do you offer to help with the washing up? If so, what do you say?
5 You are very tired and you want to leave early. How do you make this clear?

❷ Look at the pictures. What do you think the people are saying?

❸ Choose the right sentences for four of the pictures. (Be careful! In one picture the people aren't saying anything.)

1 It's getting rather late. We must be going.
2 Oh, thank you. That's very kind of you.
3 Thank you so much. It was a lovely evening.
4 That was a delicious meal.
5 You must come again soon.

WHEN DO YOU SAY IT?

❹ When would you use the following expressions? Tick [✔] all the possible answers. What else could you say? What would you say in the other situations?

1 *Excuse me.*
   a Two people are having a conversation. You want to speak to one of them.
   b You miss the bus and arrive half an hour late for school. Your teacher asks you why you are late.
   c You are in a very crowded underground train. When the train reaches your stop, there are several people between you and the door.
   d Your host family are away for the weekend and you decide to cook dinner for some friends. When the family return, you have to tell them that you have broken an expensive plate.
   e You are in a restaurant and you want to ask for the bill.

2 *You're welcome.*
   a You give a shop assistant a £5 note and a 10p coin for something that costs £1.10. He thanks you.
   b You invite some friends to dinner. They arrive two hours late.
   c You give some money to a street musician. He stops playing for a moment and thanks you.
   d Your teacher is carrying a briefcase and a cassette recorder. You open the door for her and she thanks you.
   e You are in a restaurant. A woman at the next table asks you to pass her the menu. You give it to her and she thanks you.

3 *That's OK.*
   a You pay for a newspaper with a £20 note. The newsagent gives you the change in pound coins and says he's sorry.
   b You arrange to meet a friend. He arrives an hour late and says he's sorry.
   c You are booking seats for a concert. The box office clerk offers you two seats at the back of the hall.
   d You fall on the road as you are getting off a bus. Another passenger rushes up to you and asks if you are all right.
   e A friend shows you a new sweater and asks if you like it.

4 That's right.

a   A taxi driver asks if you are a student.

b   A waiter asks if you want coffee after your meal.

c   You buy a book which costs £5.99. You give the assistant a £10 note and she gives you £4.01 change.

d   You are waiting for a bus. A woman in the queue says that the bus service is terrible.

e   You are leaving a party with some friends. One of them says: 'That was a great party, wasn't it?'

5 I'm sorry.

a   You are running to catch a train. You run quickly past a woman and knock her bag out of her hand.

b   A friend tells you that she has failed an examination.

c   A stranger comes up to you in the street and says something which you don't understand.

d   You are in a restaurant. You want to order some food, but the waiter isn't looking at you.

e   You telephone a friend, but you get the wrong number.

❺ Compare your answers with a partner. Decide how you would say the phrases in the different situations.

❻ Saying thank you and goodbye

Listen to the four conversations and answer the questions.

1   How are the conversations similar? How are they different?

2   How does the visitor thank his/her host?

3   What reason does s/he give for leaving early?

4   How does the host say 'Goodbye'?

5   How well do the people know each other?

6   How old do you think they are?

7   Put the conversations in order from the most formal to the most direct.

Conversations
A
B
C
D

❼ Going, going ... gone

Discuss these questions with other students in your class.

1   You are visiting friends for the evening. It is getting late and you want to leave. Do you:

a   say that you have to go and leave immediately?

b   say that you have to go, but stay for another fifteen minutes?

c   say that you have to go, stay for another fifteen minutes, say again that you have to go, but stay for <u>another</u> fifteen minutes?

2   Some friends are visiting you for the evening. It is getting late and you are tired. Do you:

a   tell them that you have to get up early in the morning?

b   thank them for coming and say that you hope to see them again soon?

c   start to tidy the room?

3   Look at the expressions below and put them into order from the most direct (and informal) to the most indirect (and formal).

●   It's time to go.

●   I really think we'd better be going.

●   It's time we were going.

●   Time to go.

●   It's time we went.

●   Sorry to break up the party, but we really should be going now.

❽ Put the phrases in the box below into three groups with these headings:

Formal (to people you don't know)
Semi-formal (to people you don't know very well)
Informal (to people you know quite well)

Goodbye   Thank you very much   Bye   Cheers! Thanks a lot   See you soon   See you   Bye for now I had a great time   Take care   See you later   Bye-bye Cheerio   It was very kind of you to invite me

Can you add any more words/phrases to the three lists?

❾ Choose one of the pictures and write a short conversation for it. With a partner read your conversation out to the rest of the class.

SECTION 4

WHOSE IS IT?

❶ Look at the pictures and write down all the words you think of.

❷ Work in pairs and compare your lists.

A

B

C

D

❸ Ask each other:

- what can you see in the pictures?
- what are the people doing?
- why are the people there?

❹ Listen to the conversations and write down the questions you hear.

❺ Listen again and then choose the correct answer:

1 Who do the cases belong to?
  a the first man
  b the man and the woman
 • *c* the second man

2 Who does the toy belong to?
  a the second child
 • *b* the third child
  c we can't be sure

3 Who does the coat belong to?
  a Sam
  b Pete
 • *c* we don't know

4 Who do the drinks belong to?
  a the first man
  b the second man
  c the people at the bar

❻ Complete the sentences below.

Example
It's my pen
It's mine

It's your book
It's _____

It's her watch
It's _____

It's his file
It's _____

They're our drinks
They're _____

They're your coats
They're _____

They're their tickets
They're _____

LANGUAGE PRACTICE

❼ Work in groups of four.

Use these question forms to ask each other about things in the room.

Whose …?

Is this/that …?

Are they/those …?

This/That is … isn't it?

These/Those are … aren't they?

❽ Read these expressions. Which sound more formal and which sound more relaxed? Who might say them? Who might the person be speaking to? Where might they be?

- Give it to me. It's mine. It's my teddy bear, not yours.
- Excuse me, I think you're sitting in my seat. Here is my reservation.
- I wonder if I could ask you to give me your seat. I feel air sick if I'm not next to the window.
- Is this anyone's scarf? I found it on the floor.
- What a strange pair of shorts. I don't know whether they're his or hers. Are they for men or women or are they unisex?
- Just get out of my hair and leave me alone.
- Look, he's my boyfriend, not yours.
- What's mine is mine and what's yours is yours. You can't just take whatever you want.
- Do you recognise these keys? I don't know whose they are.

❾ Now listen to the tape and say the expressions again.

❿ Work in pairs. Look at the pictures below and decide what is happening.

⓫ Who do you think the woman is phoning in the last picture? Working in pairs, write the telephone conversation.

GRAMMAR

LANGUAGE PRACTICE

Talking about the present and the past

❶ Look at the sentences below. Do they describe habits (h), routines (r), customs (c) or facts (f)? Mark each sentence with the best letter.

1   I get home at 5.30 every evening; I always have a cup of tea and put my feet up for ten minutes; I watch the six o'clock news on TV and then I make myself some supper and settle down to relax for the evening.
2   Before I write a composition, I usually try to make a plan.
3   If the service is good, people usually give the waiter about 10% as a tip.
4   Trains leave for London every hour on the hour.
5   He doesn't listen very well and he never lets me finish my sentences!
6   English teachers write long reports about individual students at the end of every school year.
7   Sunday afternoons are always the same: we have a late lunch, we go out for a long walk and then we come back and read the Sunday newspapers.
8   Most public libraries lend CDs and videotapes as well as books.

❷ Present Simple or Present Progressive? Put the verbs into the correct form.

1   I (live) in Buenos Aires, but this month I (live) in London.
2   I (study) English, but in Argentina I (work) in a bank.
3   I (stay) here for four weeks and I (work) very hard.
4   I (understand) most things that people (say) to me and my English (improve) all the time.
5   I (find) writing quite difficult, but I (enjoy) reading.
6   I (read) an interesting story at the moment and I (try) to follow it without a dictionary.
7   I (spend) every afternoon in the school's study centre and this week I (learn) a lot of new words.
8   At the weekend I usually (go) shopping , but today I (wait) for a phone call from my family.
9   My host family (spend) a week in Scotland and so I (look after) the house while they (be) away.
10   I (keep) a diary about my experiences in England and I (write) a few paragraphs every evening.

❸ Use the time phrases in the box to complete the following sentences.

five years ago   at the beginning of July
since I left university   while I've been here
for the past six weeks   every morning
when I first arrived   for the last two years
in the evening   in the last few weeks
while I'm in Cambridge   in the afternoons
when I was eighteen years old

1   I went to university _____.
2   I left university _____.
3   _____ I've had a number of different jobs.
4   However, I've worked for the same company _____ _____.
5   I arrived in Britain _____ and I've been living in Cambridge _____.
6   I'm taking a course in Business English _____ _____.
7   I have three hours of classes _____ and _____ I work for the Cambridge branch of my company.
8   After I finish my homework _____ I like to relax and watch TV.
9   _____ I couldn't speak very well, but I've been practising a lot and I think that my spoken English has really improved _____ _____.
10   I've met a lot of interesting people _____ _____ and I've really enjoyed my stay here.

❹ Pairwork Complete the questions and use them to interview your partner.

1   _____ ever eaten _____?
2   When _____ first come to Britain?
3   _____ any good films recently?
4   What _____ last weekend?
5   Did you _____ last night?
6   Haven't you ever _____?
7   Which countries _____ visited?
8   _____ you ever _____?
9   Where did _____ last year?
10   How have you _____?

54

LANGUAGE STUDY

GRAMMAR POINTS 1

● **Present simple**

Very often the present simple does not tell you anything about the present moment. It describes things which:

(a) are always true.
Example In most countries people drive on the right-hand side of the road.

(b) continue to be true.
Example They live in a small cottage in the country.

```
                . . . . _____ . . . .
    Past_____●_____
                        NOW
```

(c) are regular.
Example I work in the library for two hours every afternoon.

```
                . . . . x x x x x x x . . . .
    Past_____●_____
                        NOW
```

The present simple:
- tells us about past, present and future time.
- describes complete actions.

● **Present progressive (be + ing)**

The present progressive (often called the present continuous) is the verb form which talks about things in the present. It describes things:

(a) at the moment of speaking.
Example Oh, no! It's raining again.

```
                             x
    Past_____●_____
                        NOW
```

(b) during a present period of time.
Example I'm staying in a room at the university.

```
                . . . . x . . . .
    Past_____●_____
                        NOW
```

The present progressive:
- tells us about present time.
- describes unfinished actions.

Note It is unusual to use some verbs in the progressive:
- *like, love, dislike, hate, want, wish, believe, think, understand, hear, see, sound, need.*

GRAMMAR POINTS 2

Adverbs of frequency

Adverbs of frequency are used with the present simple and tell you *how often* something happens.

```
100%    always
 ▲      almost always
        usually
        often
        sometimes
        occasionally
 ▼      hardly ever
 0%     never
```

Always and *never* <u>always</u> come before the verb.
Other adverbs of frequency <u>usually</u> come before the verb.
<u>Sometimes</u> they can come at the beginning of the sentence. (This gives them more importance.)
Examples   I *hardly ever* eat in restaurants.
            Occasionally, I drink champagne.

GRAMMAR POINTS 3

Present perfect (have + ed)

The present perfect tells you about past experiences which are connected to the present. It describes:

(a) past experiences (at some time in the past – any time up to now).
Example I have learned a lot of new words.

```
            ? ← X → ?
    Past_____●_____
                        NOW
```

(b) past experiences (from the past to the present).
Example I have lived in London   (since 1990.
                                   (for five years.

```
                    _____→|
    Past_____x_____●_____
                        NOW
```

The present perfect:
- tells us about past time up to the present.
- describes completed and unfinished actions.

GRAMMAR POINTS 4

Present perfect simple/Present perfect progressive

The present perfect simple can show that you expect a situation to continue.
If you do not expect the situation to continue, use the present perfect progressive.
Example
I've lived in Norwich for twenty years (and I do not intend to move).
I've been living in Norwich for twenty years (but I expect to move).

The present perfect simple tells you that an action is complete.
If an action is not yet complete, use the present perfect progressive.
Example
I've done my homework. (It is finished.)
I've been doing my homework (and I'm still doing it/I haven't finished it).

The present perfect simple can describe a number of single actions.
The present perfect progressive can describe a repeated action.
Example
The phone *has rung* six times this morning (= on six separate occasions).
The phone *has been ringing* all morning (= again and again for the whole morning).

Unit 3

VOCABULARY

CLOTHES

❶ Working in pairs, look around the room. What are people wearing? List all of the items of clothing that you can see. Check your list with your partner's.

❷ Now write down the names of those items which you cannot see!

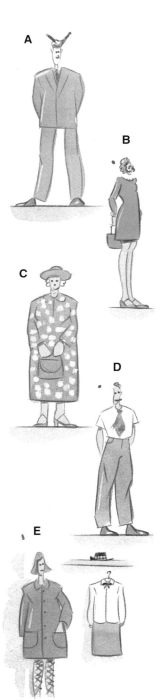

❸ Listen to these people talking about what they wear and read what they say. Match their statements with the pictures.

1   I love weddings. They are really special occasions when the men can hire morning suits and the women all put on their hats and long dresses …

2   Well I'm a policewoman so it's easy. I don't have any choice because I've got to wear my uniform for work, white blouse, black tie, black skirt and a jacket and a cap on top. Off duty you'll see me in more colourful clothes, baggy cotton dresses and things like that …

3   I don't care what I wear. I spend most of the time in tracksuits and trainers or jeans and a T-shirt, shorts in the summer …

4   For the disco, well, I get made up with lots of lipstick, some jewellery perhaps and comfortable shoes, not sandals …

5   When we go out for dinner we like to get dressed up. I usually wear a suit and tie and I'll put on some aftershave …

❹ Which word does not belong in each of the following lists? Why not? Use a dictionary to help you.

shoes
trainers, boots, sandals, clogs, flip-flops, slippers
hats
cap, top hat, baseball cap, sun hat, beret, helmet
jewellery
cufflinks, ring, necklace, bracelet, brooch, badge
underwear
petticoat, bra, tights, body suit, knickers, boxer-shorts
coats
'Barbour' waxed jacket, anorak, overcoat, mac, cape, raincoat

❺ Complete the sentences below:

-   When I go out to the theatre I like to wear …
-   I got up this morning and put on my …
-   If I had £200 to spend on clothes I would buy …
-   I would never wear …
-   My idea of a well-dressed man/woman is someone wearing …

❻ Work in pairs. Ask each other about:

-   what you like to wear
-   national costume in your country
-   which shops you like and why
-   what kind of person buys clothes in (Marks and Spencer, Laura Ashley, River Island, British Home Stores, Harrods, etc.)

FAMILY MEMBERS

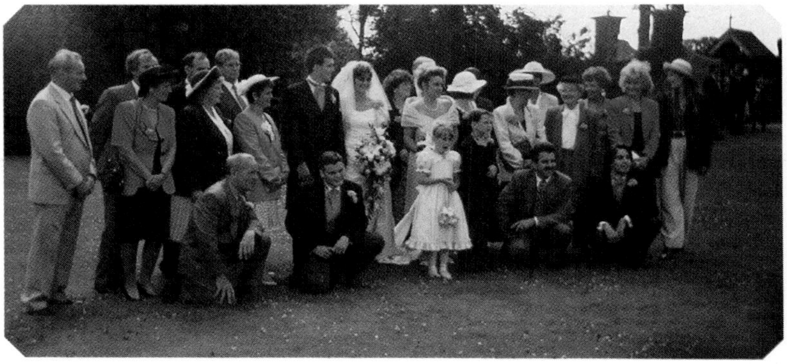

7 Work in pairs. Look at the wedding photograph. Paul Evans has married Mary Thompson. Work in pairs and decide who everyone is. How many of the following words can you use?

grandfather grandmother grandson granddaughter father mother brother sister son daughter aunt uncle cousin brother-in-law sister-in-law mother-in-law father-in-law son-in-law daughter-in-law

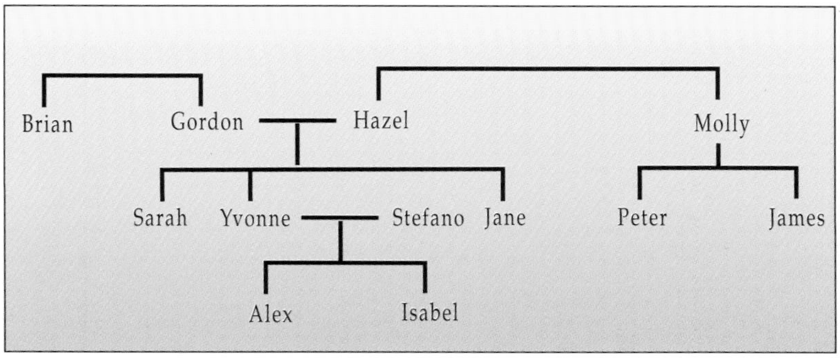

8 Look at Yvonne's family tree and listen to her explaining her family relationships, then complete the sentences below.

Yvonne is __________ to Stefano. They have two __________, Alex and Isabel. Yvonne's father has one ________________ but he didn't get married and so there are no __________ on that side of the family. Her mother has one __________ called Molly who has two __________ called Peter and James. She doesn't often see her ________________ because she lives in Australia. However, her ________________ Stefano comes from a very large ________________ with lots of ________________ and ________________ and ________________ on all sides.

9 Draw a family tree to describe your family and then explain it to your partner. What is everyone like?

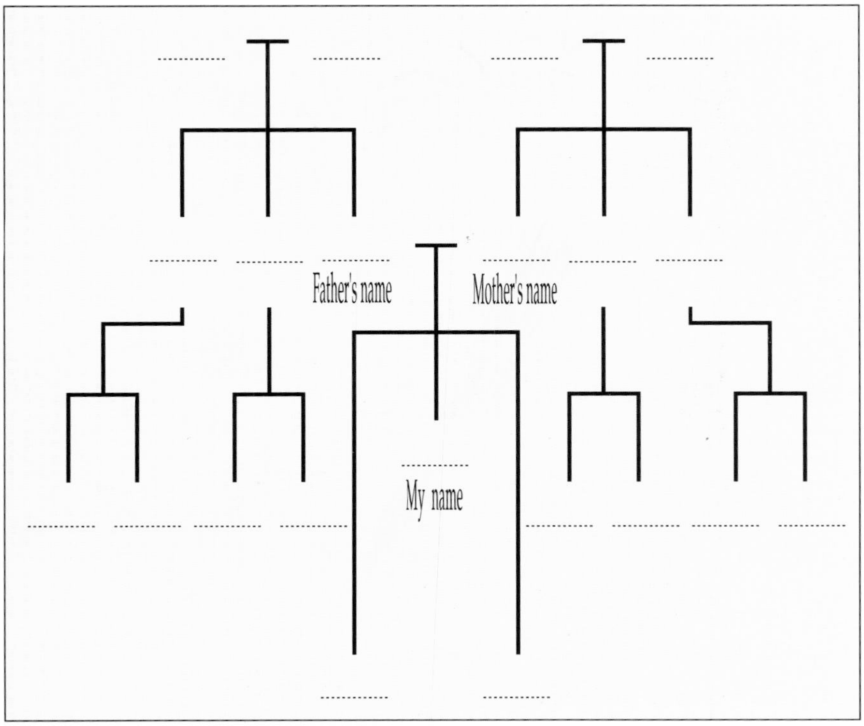

10 Write the plural for the following nouns:

Example family families

man woman person child baby niece nephew cousin

COMMON ABBREVIATIONS

11 How many of the following abbreviations (short forms) do you recognise? How many are international words?

Example Mr = Mister
PM = Prime Minister

Can you write down their full form?

Mrs Dr EU VW MP WC
UN PC AD e.g. i.e. Prof.
DOS s.a.e. PS m.p.h a.m.
p.m. mins. TV per/wk a.s.a.p.

12 Phrasal verbs

Lots of English verbs are made up (like *make + up*) by putting together one common word (*make*) and a preposition (*up*).

Work in pairs. How many verbs can you make up from the lists below? What do they mean?

make	up
get	over
put	with
find	out
give	about
hand	in

13 List any other phrasal verbs you can think of and then write them on the board.

PRONUNCIATION

VOWEL SOUNDS AND 'DOUBLE VOWEL' SOUNDS

❶ Listen to these sounds and repeat them from the tape.

❷ Listen to the sounds again and write down the words which are used as examples.

Vowel sounds

/iː/	as in _____	/ɔː/	as in _____
/ɪ/	as in _____	/ʊ/	as in _____
/e/	as in _____	/uː/	as in _____
/æ/	as in _____	/ʌ/	as in _____
/ɑː/	as in _____	/ɜː/	as in _____
/ɒ/	as in _____	/ə/	as in _____

Double vowel sounds

/eɪ/	as in _____	/ɔɪ/	as in _____
/əʊ/	as in _____	/ɪə/	as in _____
/aɪ/	as in _____	/eə/	as in _____
/aʊ/	as in _____	/ʊə/	as in _____

❸ Write down one more example word for each sound. Say it to your partner and ask her/him to show you which sound you are using.

CONSONANT SOUNDS

❹ All the sounds which are not vowels are called consonants. To make consonant sounds you use your lips, tongue, teeth and the roof of your mouth to stop or slow down the movement of air.

Listen to the tape and read at the same time:

/p/	as in pin	/ð/	as in this
/b/	as in bin	/s/	as in see
/t/	as in to	/z/	as in zoo
/d/	as in do	/ʃ/	as in show
/k/	as in come	/tʃ/	as in child
/g/	as in gum	/ʤ/	as in June
/m/	as in more	/r/	as in ring
/n/	as in nor	/l/	as in long
/ŋ/	as in bring	/w/	as in what
/f/	as in fan	/j/	as in you
/v/	as in van	/h/	as in her
/θ/	as in think	/ʒ/	as in television

❺ Now listen to the tape and put a tick beside the sounds you hear.

❻ Most of these sounds exist in your language, but some of them may not. Look back at the list and decide which sounds you will need to practise.

❼ Listen to the tape. You will hear sets of words. Repeat the words and then underline the sound that is the same in each word. (Don't worry if you don't know the meaning of the word.)

- park, apple, harp

- bark, able, rob

- wing, angry, beginning

- free, telephone, cough

- very, revision, dive

- thin, mathematics, bath

- there, neither, bathe

- spring, missing, kiss

- zed, scissors, raise

OUT OF CLASS: A SURVEY OF PEOPLE'S LIFESTYLES

This is another opportunity to use your English skills in a 'real' situation and report back to the class. You have to work in groups, prepare your questions, get information from the public, organise your information and explain your findings to the rest of the class.

The aims
- to prepare a series of questions to find out habits and customs in Britain.
- to find out more about differences in British society.
- to practise communicating in English by interviewing people 'in the street'.
- to work in groups.

The process
❶ The class should divide into five groups.
Group A: You should collect information from children and teenagers.
Group B: You should collect information from teenagers and young people.
Group C: You should collect information from people aged between twenty-five and forty.
Group D: You should collect information from people aged between forty and sixty.
Group E: You should collect information from people aged sixty or older.

❷ Decide how you can get information about the following topics:
- everyday routines (what time people get up, go to bed etc.)
- what people like to eat (where they go shopping, how much they spend on food and drink etc.)
- what people like to do for entertainment (sports, restaurants, pubs, favourite TV programmes etc.)
- where people go on holiday
- how people spend their money and where they go shopping
- how much money they need to live 'comfortably'
- what people think about politics
- what people think about religion

- Where will you go to get the information?
  - on the street, outside shops, from your host families and their friends, in cafes and pubs, by asking the managers of hotels, restaurants and shops.

- How will you stop people to ask them?
  Excuse me, I am a student from the ... school and I'm trying to find out about ..
  I wonder if I could ask you a few questions ...
- What questions will you ask?
- How long will it take?
- How will you record the information? (Notes? On a questionnaire? With a tape-recorder?)

❸ How will you organise the work? Make a list of the tasks. Decide who is going to do each task. Decide how long it will take to get the information. Do you need a group manager?

OUTSIDE THE CLASSROOM

❹ - Make sure you explain what you are doing – and why.
- Make sure you tell people who you are.
- Make sure they know how long your interview will take.
- Make sure you take good notes (or get a recording) of the information that people give you.

- Think about how you are communicating.
- Make notes of the interesting expressions you hear.
- Make a note of the successes you have and the problems you find.

BACK IN THE CLASSROOM

❺ - Put all the information together.
- Decide how you are going to present it to the rest of the class. (Blackboard? OHP? Tables of graphs and statistics? Handouts? Audio/video tape recordings?)
- Who is going to give the presentation?
- In your presentation you should:
  (a) explain the background, your 'target group' and the process involved in collecting the information;
  (b) present the information that you have collected;
  (c) explain what you think about the information and the 'lifestyles' you have described;
  (d) tell the rest of the class about how easy/difficult it was to interview people and write up any new expressions that you heard.

Unit 3

59

REVIEW

COMMUNICATION PROBLEMS

❶ Pairwork Have you been in any of the situations listed below – or in similar situations? What did you do? What did you say? What did the other person say? Think of examples and tell your partner about them.

1 You answer the telephone in your host family's house. The caller wants to leave a message, but you can't understand what s/he is saying.

2 You want to buy something in a shop, but you can't see the thing you want and you can't remember the word for it in English.

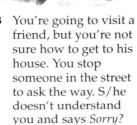

3 You're going to visit a friend, but you're not sure how to get to his house. You stop someone in the street to ask the way. S/he doesn't understand you and says *Sorry?*

4 You're at the railway station. The clerk at the enquiry desk gives you some information about times of trains, but you want to make sure that you have understood correctly.

5 Your teacher explains a difficult grammar rule, but you don't understand the example s/he has given.

❷ Listen to the conversations. Write down the phrases you hear with these meanings:

- Please repeat
- Please speak more loudly
- Please speak more slowly
- Please explain more clearly
- I want to check that I have understood
- I want something, but I don't know the right word
- I want to explain

❸ Work in groups. How many other phrases have you heard with the same meanings? Write them down under the headings in Exercise 2.

❹ Work in pairs. Choose to be the customer or the shop assistant. Plan the conversation, but don't write it. Try it and then act it out.

Customer	*Shop assistant*
You want to buy something, but you don't know the word for it in English.	You don't understand what the customer wants. Ask her/him to explain.
Explain again, but use different words.	The customer speaks too fast. Ask her/him to repeat.
Repeat your request, more slowly and clearly. Use the simplest words you can think of.	This time you think you understand, but you want to check.
Tell the assistant that s/he has understood correctly and ask what the right word is in English.	Tell the customer that you haven't got what s/he wants. Tell her/him the right word for it and where s/he can go to find it.

5 Everyday conversation

Work in groups. Think about the phrases and sentences you have heard in English conversation. Listen to these examples and add as many as you can to each list:

Greeting
Hello. How are you?
Hi! How are you getting on?
How's life with you?

Starting a conversation
What are you doing these days?
What have you been doing lately?
Have you been very busy?

Introducing a subject
Oh, by the way, ...
So, what about the ...?
Have you heard about ... ?

Continuing a conversation
That's very true.
Yes, that's right.
Mmm... I see.

Changing the subject
Yes, but did you know ...?
That reminds me ...
That's very interesting, but...

Closing a conversation
Oh, is that the time?
I must go now.
We must meet again soon.

Saying goodbye
It was nice to see you again.
See you soon, I hope.
Take care.

6 How do people start, continue and close conversations in your language? Are the phrases and sentences similar or very different? Write down some examples under the headings in Exercise 5 and then explain them in English.

UNIT REVIEW

7 Write two sentences and draw time lines to show the difference in meaning between the present simple and the present progressive.

8 Write two sentences and draw time lines to show the difference in meaning between the simple past and the present perfect.

9 New words

Look back over the Unit and write down the words which you don't remember very well.
Check the words in a dictionary and write sentences which will help you to remember the meanings.

Example

reservation
I phoned the hotel a week before we arrived to make a reservation.

10 How well are you learning? How well can you manage in English? Complete the questionnaire below.

- I can ask about people's jobs/studies. ☐
- I can talk about my job/studies. ☐
- I can ask about people's past experiences. ☐
- I can talk about my past experiences. ☐
- I can apologise for being late. ☐
- I can ask who things belong to. ☐
- I can talk about things which belong to me. ☐
- I can use polite expressions. ☐
- I can describe the members of my family. ☐
- I can describe people's clothes. ☐
- I can start a conversation. ☐
- I can close a conversation politely. ☐

Unit 3

61

SUPPLEMENTARY GRAMMAR PRACTICE EXERCISES

Talking about the present and the past

❶ Habits, routines, customs and facts
Match the words on the left with the definitions on the right:

habit   Something that a particular group of people do, sometimes on special occasions.
Example It is a _____ in Britain to send greetings cards at Christmas.

routine Something that you do very often, possibly without thinking about it.
Example He's got a _____ of closing his eyes when he's thinking.

custom   Something that is always true.
Example If you study history or science, you have to remember a lot of _____s.

fact   Something that you do regularly, every day, every week etc.
Example My daily _____ is always the same: breakfast at 7.30, the 8 o'clock news on the radio and then the 8.30 train to London.

❷ Choose words from the box to make the sentences below true for you.

| always   hardly ever   usually   sometimes |
| occasionally   never   almost always   often |

1 I _____ get up early.

2 I _____ sleep late at the weekend.

3 I _____ walk to school.

4 I _____ go to bed late.

5 I _____ read in bed.

6 I _____ watch breakfast TV.

7 I _____ arrive late for school.

8 I _____ do my homework on time.

9 I _____ speak English in the classroom.

10 I _____ use an English-English dictionary.

❸ Correct the sentences below.

1 I am listening to the news at six o'clock every evening.
2 I go often to the cinema.
3 He is wanting a new job.
4 She is usually coming late to school.
5 He gives me a lift home always.

❹ Use the prompts to make questions.

1 you/ever/be/to America?
2 he/buy/any presents/yet?
3 Maria/already/write/to her parents?
4 you/see/*Jurassic Park*?
5 Thomas and Peter/leave/school?
6 you/hear/the news/today?
7 they/learn/the present perfect/yet?
8 you/feel/cold/in Britain?
9 the plane/take off/yet?
10 prices/go up/this year?

❺ Simple past or present perfect? Put the verbs into the correct form.

1 I (go) to the cinema on Saturday.
2 The weather (be) awful this summer.
3 I (not finish) my homework yet.
4 (.........) you (read) *The Third Man*?
5 I (not see) you since we (meet) in London.
6 (........) you (remember) to post my letter?
7 That (be) the best meal I (have) for ages.
8 I (give up) smoking on 1 January.
9 I (not have) a cigarette since the beginning of the year.
10 (........) you hear the news last night?

❻ Use short answers in the present perfect to answer the questions below. Add more information, as in the example.

Example
Have you ever been to the Caribbean?
Yes, *I have*. I *went* there ..... years ago.
    or
No, *I haven't*, but I *have been* to ....

Have you ever ...
 1 ... been skiing?
 2 ... broken your leg?
 3 ... seen a Shakespeare play?
 4 ... been to Scotland?
 5 ... drunk English beer?
 6 ... lost your passport?
 7 ... eaten Indian food?
 8 ... read a book in English?
 9 ... played cricket?
 10 ... swum in the English Channel?

❼ Correct the sentences below.

 1 Did the train leave already?
 2 Have you been to York last week?
 3 I am a student since 1993.
 4 They have visited Edinburgh two years ago.
 5 The plane took off before five minutes.

❽ Choose the present perfect simple or the present perfect progressive to complete the following sentences.

 1 I (work) as a teacher since I left university.
 2 For the last few months I (think) about changing my job.
 3 I (not decide) yet, but I (meet) more and more people who (change) their careers.
 4 I (read) several newspaper articles about retraining and I (look) at the job advertisements every day for the past few weeks.
 5 I (not find) the right job yet, but I (decide) that I (teach) for too long.

Unit 3

UNIT 4

PLANNING AHEAD

In this unit you will find:

- language practice to help you
  - ask what someone did;
  - ask what it was like;
  - ask what someone is going to do;
  - ask what someone will do;

- vocabulary to help you talk about
  - education;
  - the media;
  - the weather;
  - describing things using adjectives;

- Pronunciation work on
  - word stress;
  - sentence stress;

- your 'Out of class' project, which is a choice from:
  - telling stories;
  - making a visual collage of the school;
  - making a game;
  - making a scrapbook of your experiences in Britain;
  - making a souvenir video;

- grammar points to teach you about:
  - talking about the future;
  - using the present simple and present progressive to talk about the future;
  - using *will* to talk about the future;
  - using *going to* to talk about the future.

SECTION 1

WHAT DID YOU DO?

❶ What are these things, places and people called in your language? Do you know the words in English?

❷ Match the two groups of pictures.

❸ **Pairwork**   Talk about the pictures. Have you ever been to any of these places? Is there anything similar in your country? Which place would you like to visit? Why?

❹ Listen and read. Identify the pictures which go with each conversation.

a
- What did you do at the weekend?
- Oh, I had a great time, I went to the funfair.
- What was it like?
- Brilliant! I loved the big wheel but it was really frightening and I spent *so* much money!

b
- Where were you on Saturday? We waited for you, you know.
- Ah, well, umm, sorry about that.
- What happened to you?
- Well, my host family took me to the races. It was really interesting. I placed a bet and I won twenty pounds.

c
- What did you do at the weekend? Did you go anywhere nice?
- Yes, we went to Winchester for the day.
- What did you do?
- Well, we went round the cathedral – it's very big and very old, and it's got a famous choir – then we went to the castle and saw King Arthur's Round Table in the Great Hall! After that we had a picnic by the river. It was great!

❺ **Pairwork**   Ask each other about how you spent your free time.

What did you do at/on .....?
Did you .....?
How was your weekend/evening?

Write short conversations based on the answers. Act them out for the rest of the class.

❻ Look at these adjectives. Group them in order from most positive to most negative.

great   awful   fantastic   brilliant   horrible really good   really bad   all right   nothing special amazing   terrible

Positive	Negative

❼ Read and think about the missing words. Try to guess who is speaking.

A

Well, I was the longest -serving _____ _____ of Great Britain in the twentieth century. And that's not all. I was the _____ _____ Prime Minister ever. I was born in a small town called Grantham. I went to Oxford University and I had two children. I was _____ up to believe in freedom and _____ _____ . I knew how to look after money and I believe that people should be free to choose how to spend their money. I disagree with _____ . I stopped being Prime Minister in 1990. My name is ...

B

I was not very good at looking after money. I was a _____. I wrote _____, lots of them. They were very popular and they were _____ into many other languages. I wanted to help the _____. I believed in the reform of education and wanted to stop _____. I hated the selfish habits of the middle classes who didn't think about other people. Above all else, I wanted to help children. I wrote about things like this in *Oliver Twist* and *Great Expectations*. My name is ...

C

I am a _____. People think I lived in the fourteenth century. I loved a woman called Maid Marian and I _____against the Sheriff of Nottingham. I lived in the forest and I _____money from the rich to give to the poor. People like to make _____about me. In fact, they made one in 1990 with Kevin Costner and called me 'Prince of _____'. My name is …

❽ Now listen and complete the passages. Were your guesses correct?

❾ **Pairwork**   With a partner, think about the questions you would like to ask each person. Compare your questions with another pair.

Why did you ...?
Did you want to ...?
What did you do when ... ?
Did you ever ... ?

Unit 4

WHAT WAS IT LIKE?

❶ Work in pairs and ask each other about the pictures.

- Have you seen any of these things?
- Where did you see them?
- What is the connection between the pictures?

❷ Look at the picture stories below. Who are the people? Where are they? What is happening? Can you tell the rest of the class?

Garage Appointments
Tell us what you think about this garage
ADDITIONAL COMMENTS ....
NAME OFGARAGE ....
ADDRESS OF GARAGE ....
DATE OF SERVICE/REPAIR ....
INVOICE NUMBER ....
CUSTOMER NAME ....
CUSTOMER ADDRESS ....
CUSTOMER SIGNATURE ....
AA MEMBER YES ☐ NO ☐

If you enjoyed your meal, please tell your friends. If you didn't, please tell the management.

If you are not absolutely satisfied with any of our products, please return it within seven days of purchase for a full refund.

WOULD YOU DESCRIBE THE SERVICE WE HAVE JUST GIVEN YOU AS **EXCELLENT**
YES ■   NO ■
Dear Customer
Out first priority is to provide our Customers with an EXCELLENT service.
Safety and quality are built in to all the services we offer, and hopefully we successfully provide you with the reliable, efficient and safe service you demand.
has this commitment to Safety and Quality. However, in the end it is YOUR appreciated if you could spend a little of your time to complete and good or bad, of the standard of service you have just
card, and I will contact you

Your Name ....
Address ....
Telephone No. (Home) .... (Business)............
Model ....
Registration No. .... Job No./
Invoice No.
Please delete as appropriate
1. Did our Reception staff greet you by name? ....YES/NO
2. Were you welcomed with a smile? ....YES/NO
3. Did our Reception staff deal with you promptly ....YES/NO
4. Was the work requested completed to your satisfaction?
............YES/NO
If not, why?............
5. Did we complete all the work requested?............YES/NO
6. Was the work completed on time? ....YES/NO

❸ Are these sentences true or false? Look at the pictures and decide.

A **1** The man and the woman are both enjoying the first course.
   2 She likes her main course, but he doesn't like his at all.
   3 He is enjoying his dessert, but she thinks that hers tastes awful.
   4 They both think that the bill is very reasonable.

B **1** The man is looking forward to seeing the film, but the woman doesn't want to see it.
   2 She looks bored when the film begins, but he looks quite pleased.
   3 She thinks the film is very frightening, but he is enjoying it.
   4 He hated the film, but she enjoyed it.

❹ Now write true sentences for all the pictures.

❺ Pairwork What do you think the two couples say to each other when they leave the restaurant and the cinema? Write down the conversations.

❻ Now act out your conversations for the rest of the class.

❼ Read the scripts below and think about the missing words.

A *Man:* How did you _____ the meal, darling?
Woman: Well, the first course was very _____, but I didn't _____ much of the main course and I didn't _____ the dessert at all.
Man: Oh, I'm sorry your meal was so _____. Mine was absolutely _____. Everything was just _____ – except the bill!
Woman: Yes, it was rather _____, wasn't it?

B *Woman:* So, what did you _____ of the film?
Man: I'm afraid I didn't _____ it very much. It wasn't really my _____ of thing. You _____ it, though, didn't you?
Woman: Yes, I _____ it. I thought the photography was _____ and the acting was _____. Why didn't you _____ it?
Man: Well, quite honestly, I thought it was all rather _____. It was too _____, too _____ and not at all _____.
Woman: Really? Is that why you didn't want to watch it?

❽ Listen to the recordings and complete the scripts with the words you hear.

❾ Pairwork With your partner, choose one of the situations below and decide which character you will play. Plan the conversation, but don't write it. Practise it and then act it out for the class.

Situation A

Student
You have just returned home after three weeks in Britain. You had a wonderful time and you want to tell your friend about all the interesting places you visited.

Friend
You have never been to Britain, but you think that the pictures look very attractive. You ask your friend lots of questions about the places that s/he visited.

Situation B

Student
You have just been to a modern art exhibition with a friend. You thought it was terrible. You know that your friend liked it. You don't want him/her to know how much you disliked it.

Friend
You invited your friend to visit a modern art exhibition with you. You know that s/he didn't like it very much. S/he says it was all right, but you think s/he is just being polite.

❿ Now take turns with your partner to ask each other about places you have visited in Britain and what you saw there.

Examples

What did you think of _____? It was wonderful.
Did you like _____? It was all right.
Did you enjoy _____? It was rather
How did you like _____? disappointing.

⓫ Group the expressions below under the following headings:

very positive [✔✔] positive [✔] neutral [▬]
negative [✘] very negative [✘✘]

- It wasn't too bad at all.
- I wasn't too keen on it.
- It wasn't terribly good.
- It was all right, I suppose.
- It was fairly good.
- I didn't care for it very much.
- It was OK.
- It wasn't the best thing I've ever seen.
- I quite liked it.
- I thought it was terrific.
- I've never seen anything worse.
- It was rather good, actually.

⓬ Now listen carefully to the voices on the tape and check your answers to the last exercise.

⓭ Look at these examples.

very cold
rather expensive
The meal was **fairly** good   The meal was **delicious**.
quite nice
a bit overcooked.

Some adjectives, like 'delicious' in the example, have meanings which are 100% – you can't change their meaning with words like 'very' or 'fairly'.
Can you find the other 100% adjectives in the box below?

fantastic	beautiful	enjoyable	interesting
surprising	boring	terrible	stupid	awful
excellent	difficult	positive	impossible
amazing	wonderful	nice	marvellous

Unit 4

SECTION 3

WHAT ARE YOU GOING TO DO?

❶ Look at the pictures. Which of these do you think each person is thinking about?

- last-minute shopping
- going back home
- future job plans
- changing her/his habits for the better
- deciding to do something

❷ Read the replies. Try to guess what the situations and the questions might be.

A

I'm going to be a doctor.

B

I'm going to ask Elena for a dance.

C

I'm going to stop smoking.

D

I'm going to go skiing.

E

I'm going to do some last-minute shopping.

❸ Listen to the conversations and check your guesses. Write down the main questions you hear.

❹ What else did the people say? Listen again and make notes of other phrases that you hear.

❺ Use the prompts below to make questions like those on the tape.

1 what/you/going/do/tonight?
2 be/you/going/study/English/when/go/home?
3 where/you/going/go/before/leave?
4 what sort of presents/you/going/buy/for your family?
5 where/you/going/buy/the presents?
6 what/be/first thing/you/going/do/when/go/ home?
7 who/you/going/remember/after/the course?
8 what/you/going/tell/your friends/about Britain?
9 when/you/going/come back to Britain?
10 what/you/going/do/when/finish the course?

❻ Pairwork   Now use the questions to find out about your partner's plans.

❼ Listen to these expressions and repeat them, using the same intonation.

- What do you think you're going to do with your life? You can't just carry on living at home.
- I'm really going to try hard next time. I'm going to revise and I'm going to pass the exam.
- What are you going to do tonight? Are you going to go to the party or are you going to stay in?

❽ Who do you think might be saying these things? Who are they speaking to?

❾ Pairwork   Look at the pictures below. Who are the people? Where are they? What might they be talking about? With your partner, write something about each picture.

❿ Now decide what is going to happen in each situation. Write three sentences explaining what happens next and then read your sentences to the rest of the class.

SECTION 4

WHAT WILL YOU DO?

❶ Look at the pictures and list all the words you think of for each one.

❷ **Pairwork** Compare your lists with your partner's.

❸ Ask each other:

- Have you seen/heard...?
- Have you got...?
- Do you enjoy...?

❹ Listen to the conversations. What are the students very sure/fairly sure/not sure about? Make notes under the headings for conversations A, B, C and D.

Very sure
A
B
C
D

Fairly sure
A
B
C
D

Not sure
A
B
C
D

❺ How would you say these expressions? Which sound more formal and which sound more relaxed? Who do you think is speaking? Who do you think they are speaking to? Where do you think they are?

- Will you be free on Wednesday afternoon?
- I'll see you soon.
- I don't know. Maybe I will – maybe I won't.
- I think you'll like it.
- The manager will see you now.
- I hope it won't rain.
- It will just take a few minutes.
- Where will you stay?

❻ Now listen to the tape and say the expressions again.

WRITING

❼ Pairwork With your partner, choose one of the situations below and write a short conversation. When you have finished, act it out for the rest of the class.

A Two students are discussing their future careers. One of them has very clear ideas about what kind of job s/he wants to have. The other has lots of different ideas, but hasn't finally decided.

B Two students are planning a surprise birthday party for a friend. They don't want their friend to know anything about the party until the last moment. They discuss a 'timetable' for the early part of the evening.

C Two friends are going on holiday together. One of them has already decided where they will stay and what they will do. When they discuss these plans, they disagree about some of them.

❽ Pairwork Match the symbols with the words in the box. Then take turns with your partner to ask and answer questions about the weather.

Examples

- What will you do if it rains?   I'll take an umbrella.
- What will the weather be like in July?   It will probably be sunny.

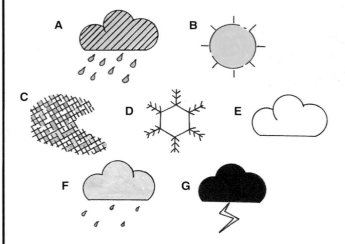

sunny cloudy foggy snow showers wet
storms rain bright

❾ What is the first thing you will do when you return home after this course? Write your answer on a slip of paper. Now put the slips for the whole class in a box, mix them up and take turns to pick one out without looking. (If you choose your own slip, put it back and take another one.) Read what is written on your paper and go round the class asking 'What's the first thing you will do when you get home?' until you find the person who gave the answer you have.

Unit 4

GRAMMAR

LANGUAGE PRACTICE

TALKING ABOUT THE FUTURE

❶ Look at the sentences below. Underline the words that refer to the future.

1   I leave at 6.30 in the morning.
2   I'm packing my bags this evening.
3   I'm going to get the early train.
4   I'll be in London at 9.30.
5   I'll probably take a taxi to the airport.
6   It will take me about an hour to check in, go through customs and do some duty-free shopping.
7   The plane is scheduled to leave at 12.00.
8   So that's it. I'm leaving tomorrow.
9   I will send you all postcards.
10 I won't forget you.
11 I'll be back.

Present simple or present progressive?

❷ Put the verbs in the correct form.

1   You (have) an appointment with Mr Thompson at 10.00 a.m., then you (see) Ms Winstanley from the bank at 11.00 a.m. Lunch with the Board of Directors (be) at 1.00 p.m. and I've ordered a taxi for you.
2   We (move) to Somerset next month because Jean (start) a new job in Wells.
3   The flight (be) at six tomorrow and you (arrive) in Paris at seven, local time.
4   I (speak) at a conference in Brighton next week so I (not come) to the club on Saturday. Please give them my apologies.
5   She is such a busy person. In August she (go) to the Edinburgh Festival, in September she (open) a new restaurant in Norwich and then in October she (have) a baby!

'Will' or 'going to'?

❸ Put the verbs in the correct form.

1   'I (be) an airline pilot when I grow up and I (fly) big jumbo jets', the little girl told her mother.
2   'Bye for now, I (see) you at Roger's tonight. I (be) there at about eight.
3   The car needs a service. I (take) it to the garage this afternoon.
4   Look at those black clouds. It (rain). I (take) the washing in.
5   I know it's getting late but I (finish) this report before I go to bed.
6   He (play) golf next weekend.
7   I (go) to Turkey for two months in the summer.
8   I (meet) you at the café at six o'clock.

❹ Choose one of these verbs to complete the sentences below:

plan   want   hope   expect   think

1   I _____ to stay with this company for another year and then I _____ to get a job in London.
2   I _____ you won't have any problems in your new house. I don't _____ you will.
3   I _____ I'll come back to Britain next year but I'm not sure.
4   I _____ to see you again. I _____ you will phone me.
5   The weather is so bad, I don't _____ many people will come to the garden party.

Future plans and appointments

❺ Fill out your diary for the week. Include things which you want to do as well as things you have to do.

	MON	TUES	WED	THURS	FRI	SAT	SUN
Morning							
Lunch							
Afternoon							
Evening							

❻ Pairwork   Take turns to ask questions about what your partner is going to do each day.

❼ Talk to as many different people as you can. Find out what their plans are and ask them to join you in what you are doing. Try to find two people to join you every evening.

Are you free on ...?   I'm free/not free on ...
What are you doing on ...?   I'm –ing.
Are you going on ...?   I'm going to ...
Will you join me on ...?   Yes/No.

LANGUAGE STUDY

TALKING ABOUT THE FUTURE

- There is no future tense in English. There are different ways of talking about the future.

- There is no clear difference between *will* and *shall*. In speech, they are nearly always contracted to *-ll*.

- *Going to* is used more often than *will* in spoken English.

GRAMMAR POINTS 1

Present simple

- The present simple is used to talk about fixed future arrangements. It is used with clear markers of time.

```
                                  X (a fixed point in the future)
Past _____•_____
                     NOW
```

Examples
The train *leaves* at six fifteen.
You *have* a meeting at ten, then you *see* your first client at eleven.
I *leave* the company on the 28th of the month.

GRAMMAR POINTS 2

Present progressive

- The present progressive is used to talk about future arrangements and activities.

```
                          XXXXX (an 'on-going' period
                                 of activity in the future)
Past _____•_____
                     NOW
```

Examples
I'm travelling home next week.
We are moving to Italy next month.
He's playing tennis on Saturday afternoon.

GRAMMAR POINTS 3

Will

- *Will* + infinitive of the verb is used to describe things you expect to happen.

Examples
I'll get the first train in the morning. So I'll be in London by nine o'clock.
I'll get a well-paid job when I leave university.
I'll finish this report and then I'll come to bed.

- The negative form of the *will* future is made using *will* + *not*. In speech and in writing, this form is usually contracted to *won't*.

Examples
We haven't got any money, so we won't be going on holiday this year.
I won't visit you next week, I'll be too busy.

GRAMMAR POINTS 4

Going to

- *Going to* + infinitive of the verb is used to describe plans and future intentions. These may happen to a fixed point in time or over a longer period in the future.

```
                                  X (XXXX.....)
Past _____•_____
                     NOW
```

Examples
I'm going to buy a new car next month.
We're going to get married in June.
Are you going to visit the Hermitage Museum when you go to St Petersburg?
I don't know what I'll do when I leave college – I'm just going to wait and see what turns up.

GRAMMAR POINTS 5

- There are some important verbs which are always used to refer to the future. They include:

plan	want	hope	expect	think

Examples
I'm planning a holiday in Greece next year.
She wants to go to university eventually.
He's hoping to get into the football team.
We expect them to invite us to the wedding, of course.
They're thinking of joining the Youth Hostels Association.

Unit 4

VOCABULARY

A EDUCATION

❶ Use the words in the box to complete the sentences below.

> secondary primary nursery higher middle
> fees degree public college state

1 Before the age of five many children go to a
   _____ school or playgroup.

2 Then, when they are five years old, they go to a
   _____ school.

3 From eight to twelve they move to a _____
   school.

4 They have to stay at _____ school until they are
   sixteen.

5 Many students stay at school until they are eighteen
   because they want to go on to a _____ or
   university for further or _____ education.

6 Most _____ courses at university last for three
   or four years.

7 Some people pay very high _____ to send their
   children to private schools.

8 It is strange that these private schools are called
   _____ schools.

9 Most parents still prefer to send their children to
   _____ schools.

❷ Work in groups. Discuss your answers to these
questions.

1 What is the *school leaving age* in your country?
2 Do you get a *report* at the end of the year?
3 Does the teacher check the *register* every morning?
4 How many different *subjects* do you have to study?
5 Do all the students come together for an *assembly*
  every morning?
6 How many lessons do you have on your weekly
  timetable?
7 How many *periods* are there in your school day?
8 Do you have a *half-day*?
9 Do you have any *free periods* for study?
10 Does the school give you any time for *revision* before
   an exam?

B DICTIONARIES AND LANGUAGE LEARNING

❸ Change the words in capital letters to complete the
sentences.

Example

Read, speak and *write* are all *irregular* verbs.
                                              REGULAR

1 Many students like to write down a
  new word with a _____ in their
  own language.   TRANSLATE

2 They use a dictionary to look up the
  _____ of a new word.   MEAN

3 But knowing a word means more than
  just understanding the _____
  in the dictionary.   DEFINE

4 Most people use dictionaries to check
  their _____.   SPELL

5 A dictionary also uses a special alphabet
  to give you the _____ of a word. PRONOUNCE

6 Words are arranged from A to Z in the
  dictionary in _____ order.   ALPHABET

7 When you look something up in a
  dictionary, there are _____ like *vb*
  and *adj*, which show you what kind of
  word it is.   ABBREVIATE

8 You can usually find a list of these in
  the _____ at the beginning of the
  dictionary.   INTRODUCE

9 Learners' dictionaries sometimes use
  an _____ to show you what
  something looks like.   ILLUSTRATE

10 A picture is often easier to understand
   than a _____.   DESCRIBE

C THE MEDIA

❹ Group the words/phrases in three boxes under the
headings *newspapers*, *radio* and *TV*. (Some of the words
may belong to more than one group.)

> channel headline station article broadcast
> colour supplement viewer phone-in
> disc jockey reviewer announcer screen tune in
> soap opera feature documentary journalist
> director studio editor remote control
> foreign correspondent subtitles cartoon print
> the box live (adj.)

76

Newspapers

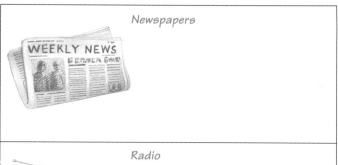

Radio

TV

D THE WEATHER

❺ Listen to the weather forecast and draw the symbols in the right places on the map. Make notes of any other words or phrases that you hear for describing different kinds of weather.

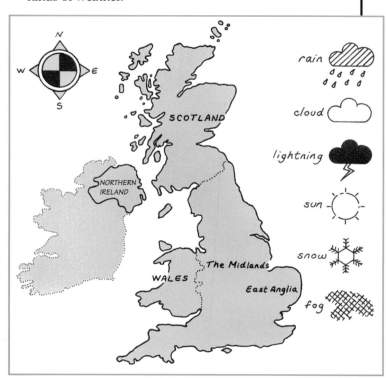

E ADJECTIVES

❻ Think back over your stay in England. What were the best things that happened to you? What did you enjoy? What were the worst things? What did you dislike?

Work in groups. Take it in turns to talk about your experiences. Each person must use the next adjective in the circle, starting with *fantastic*.

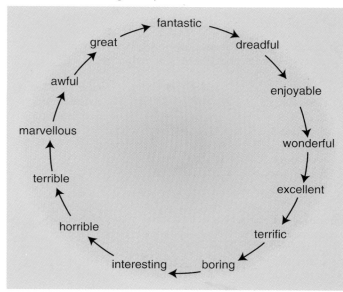

F PHRASAL VERBS

❼ Use your own ideas to complete the following sentences. (The first one has been done for you.)

1 At the beginning of the course our teacher gave out *maps of the city.*

2 When I am reading in English I always look up

_____.

3 Once or twice a week I like to look at my notebook and go through _____.

4 If I want to practise a new word, I often make up

_____.

5 When I'm doing my homework, I often find it difficult to work out _____.

6 During the lesson I always write down

_____.

7 I want the teacher to correct my mistakes and to point out _____.

8 When I am writing in English, I often leave out

_____.

9 When we have a class test, I don't always have time to finish off _____.

10 I enjoy doing exercises where we have to fill in

_____.

Unit 4

PRONUNCIATION

STRESS

WORD STRESS

❶ Listen to the words on tape and repeat them in the pauses. Listen carefully for the main stress.

person   travellers   conversation
nephew   similar   reservation
necklace   recognise   examination
restaurant   suitcases
trainers
weddings
tracksuits
Christmas

❷ Now look at the words and think about how to say them. Mark the stressed syllable.

Example

'person
'travellers
conver'sation

❸ Pairwork   Write down five new words that you have learned. Ask your partner to mark the stressed syllable and then say the word.

❹ Some words change their meaning when the stress is moved from one syllable to another. When the stress is on the first syllable it is usually a noun or adjective and when it is on the second syllable it is usually a verb. Listen to the example.

Example

I work for an 'export company.
I ex'port motorbikes and tyres.

Now read these sentences and decide where to put the stress on the words in italics.

- She gave me a *present* for my birthday.
- I want to *import* French wine and cheese.
- Can you help me with my *project*?
- *Refuse* is another word for rubbish or garbage.
- They have a small market garden, and *produce* mainly salad vegetables and strawberries.
- They will *present* me with my prize on Friday.
- I need the company sales figures to *project* next month's profit.
- I *refuse* to help you again because you never help me.
- They sell their *produce* to the local supermarket.
- I'm in the *import*/export business.

❺ Listen and check your answers. Repeat the sentences in the pauses.

SENTENCE STRESS

❻ Generally, the most important words in a sentence carry the main stress. Listen to these news headlines and write down the important words that you hear.

❼ Look at these sentences. Mark the syllables which you expect to carry the stress.

- I live in Paris.
- I'm leaving tomorrow.
- I'll wear a green dress.
- The children loved their ice cream.
- Can you pass me the salt, please?
- Jane didn't come to the party.
- It rained all the time.
- John wants to go home.

❽ Now listen and check your answers.

❾ The meaning of a sentence can be changed by moving the main stress to a different syllable. Listen to this simple sentence and explain how the meaning changes. Where might the person be? Who might he be speaking to? Who else might be there? What does he mean?

I <u>love</u> you.
I love <u>you</u>.

OUT OF CLASS: FINAL PROJECT

This is your chance to choose a project which you can direct to make the best use of the language skills you have acquired. You should use the skills you have developed working in groups, getting information and presenting your findings to the rest of the class.

You can either choose one of the projects here or develop one of your own.

1 Stories
- Choose a situation: arrival in Britain; the first day in the school; the worst day in Britain etc.
- Interview other students in the class, in the school or other students in the town.
- Choose the best stories and make them into a booklet.
- Illustrate the booklet and photocopy it for the other students in the class.

3 Game
- Go to toyshops, bookshops, (e.g. WH Smith) etc. and look at the board games that are available.
- Use some of the ideas to develop a simple board game based on the experiences of a student studying English in Britain.
- Make the game and try it out with others in the class.

4 Scrapbook
- Collect as much information relating to your stay in Britain as you can.
- Add it to the ideas and stories you have in your diary.
- Use some of the material from projects you have done before.
- Present it to the rest of the class as a scrapbook of experiences which you can talk about.

5 Souvenir video
- Make a video record of your class and your experiences.
- Collect short video diaries from everyone in the class.
- Film the school and the staff.
- Film the best-known and most popular places in the town.
- Show your video to the rest of the class.

2 A visual collage of the school
- Collect interviews from people involved with the school. Collect their opinions and select the best quotations. Write them down.
- Collect as much publicity material about the school as you can, and cut up text and pictures which you want to use.
- Collect written c.v.s from students, and job profiles and photographs from staff. Choose the ones you want to use.
- Arrange all of the material into a collage which summarises life at the school and present it to the rest of the class in the form of a poster.

Unit 4

REVIEW

WHAT HAVE YOU LEARNED ABOUT ENGLISH?

Think back to the beginning of your course. What new things have you learned? What did you find difficult in English before? What do you find easier now? Think about the language you know and how you are able to use it in different situations.

LANGUAGE SKILLS

❶ Tick [✔] the statements below which are true for you and add your own ideas.

Listening
I can ...
- understand simple conversations when I know something about the subject ☐
- listen to the news on radio or TV and understand the most important information ☐
- get the information I need from announcements (e.g. in a railway station) ☐
- _____
- _____
- _____

Reading
I can ...
- understand the general meaning of stories in the newspapers ☐
- enjoy reading simple stories without using the dictionary ☐
- find information I need in advertisements, guidebooks etc. ☐
- _____
- _____
- _____

Speaking
I can ...
- answer questions about where I come from, what I do, etc. ☐
- ask for information in shops, offices, etc. ☐
- ask people to repeat or explain when I don't understand ☐
- _____
- _____
- _____

Writing
I can ...
- write simple notes and messages ☐
- write correct information about myself ☐
- write short letters to friends ☐
- _____
- _____
- _____

GRAMMAR AND VOCABULARY

❷ Use the boxes to make notes about grammar and vocabulary. In the top half of each each box, make lists of the grammar points (e.g. the Present Perfect) and areas of vocabulary (e.g. colours) which you feel quite sure about. In the bottom half of the boxes, make lists of the grammar and vocabulary which you are not so sure about.

Grammar

✔

?

Vocabulary

✔

?

SITUATIONS

❸ How sure do you feel in different situations in English? Put a tick in the column which is true for you.

	I always know what to say	I am sometimes not sure what to say	I don't know what to say
Asking for directions	☐	☐	☐
Travelling by bus/train/taxi	☐	☐	☐
Shopping	☐	☐	☐
Ordering a meal in a restaurant	☐	☐	☐
Asking for information	☐	☐	☐
Meeting new people	☐	☐	☐
Having dinner with your host family	☐	☐	☐
Talking about:			
- yourself and your family	☐	☐	☐
- general subjects (the weather, places to go, etc.)	☐	☐	☐
- your school/job	☐	☐	☐
- special interests (e.g. sports, hobbies)	☐	☐	☐
Giving your opinions (e.g. about stories in the news)	☐	☐	☐

HOW WILL YOU CONTINUE LEARNING?

❹ **Pairwork**   Exchange your answers to Exercises 1 -3. What advice would you give to your partner to improve her/his English in the future? Discuss the suggestions below. Which of them are possible for you? What else can you do if they are not possible? Add your own ideas.

- Listen to *English by Radio* on the BBC World Service
- Listen to songs in English
- Go to see films in English
- Watch videos in English
- Use your local British Council library
- Look at newspapers or news magazines in English
- Find a magazine about your special interest (e.g. football, rock music)
- Write letters to your host family
- Talk to English-speaking visitors
- Use grammar and vocabulary practice books

WHAT HAVE YOU LEARNED ABOUT LIFE IN BRITAIN?

Sights and sounds

❺ Think back over your stay in Britain. Think about the things you have seen and heard. What was unusual or surprising? When you tell your friends about your stay, what are things you will remember? Make notes.

Way of life

❻ Think about the people you have met. Think about the way they behaved in different situations. Write adjectives to describe them.

❼ Work in groups. Compare your answers to Exercises 5 and 6. What are the most popular images and ideas about Britain and the British in your group? Prepare a poster to show to the rest of the class.

Unit 4

UNIT REVIEW

WRITING

❽ How did you spend your free time during the course? What did you do? What was it like? Write about the most interesting things.

❾ What arrangements have you made for your journey home? What plans have you got for the next few weeks? What do you think will happen to you over the next few months? Complete the sentences opposite.

- I'm _____
  _____
- I'm going to _____
  _____
- I'll probably _____
  _____
  _____

SUPPLEMENTARY GRAMMAR PRACTICE EXERCISES

❶ Make questions from the prompts, using the present simple or present progressive tense.

1 when/I/have the meeting/with the Board of Directors
2 Why/you/move/to Somerset
3 when/Jean/start/new job
4 what time/be/flight/tomorrow
5 what/speak about/in Cambridge
6 what/Alice/do/in Edinburgh
7 when/new restaurant/open
8 when/Alice/have/her baby
9 when/they/go/on holiday
10 when/new term/start
11 how/you/travel/home
12 she/play/badminton/next Saturday

❷ What are your plans? Fill in the gaps and write down your schedule.

When does the course end?

My course _____ on _____

and I _____ home on _____

How are you travelling?

I _____ the bus/train/plane from

_____ to _____

Then I _____ .

When do you arrive?

I _____ in _____ at

_____

❸ Choose a suitable verb to complete the sentences below.

1 I _____ the early-morning bus so that I

_____ in Birmingham before nine o'clock.

2 She _____ at the station, then we _____ to

her house to get changed for the party.

3 What _____ when the bank _____ give you

any more money?

4 I _____ you at six o'clock outside the library.

Make sure you _____ there on time!

5 I _____ her when I catch her. She _____ be

sorry!

6 She (not) _____ to the party. I asked her and she

said 'no'.

7 I've spent all my money so I (not) _____ any

presents for my family.

8 The performance _____ in two minutes. They're

late. They (not) _____ seats.

9 I asked her to marry me, but her parents (not)

_____ . They say she's too young.

10 When _____ you _____ into your new

house?

❹ Follow the example below and make up your own sentences.

Example
Alice is in Edinburgh through August and so she won't be able to meet you in London.

1 I'm flying home tomorrow and so ...
2 I had a bad time at that restaurant and so ...
3 Sadly, her parents don't want us to get married and so ...
4 They are moving to London next week and so ...
5 My contract with this company ends tomorrow and so ...
6 You won't help me and so I ...
7 The course ends on Friday and so we ...
8 I forgot to pack my swimming costume and so ...
9 She's going to stop smoking on Friday and so ...
10 His company has sent him on a computer course and so ...

❺ Write answers for the questions below.

1 What are you doing tonight?
2 What are you going to do next summer?
3 What will you tell your friends about when you get home?
4 How will you practise your English when you are back at home?
5 What time do you arrive home?

6 How are you travelling home?
7 Who will you remember from the course?
8 Where are you going to go at the weekend?
9 Will you continue to study English?
10 What are you doing tomorrow?

❻ Complete the dialogues.

Example
Person A   What are you going to do on Saturday?
Person B   I'm going to the opera in the park.
Person A   What will you do if it rains?
Person B   I'll take my large umbrella.

1 Person A   ....this evening?

Person B   ....stay at home and finish my

homework.

Person A   ....if you finish early?

Person B   ....watch the television.

2 Person A   How...............................to London?

Person B   ....the train.

Person A   ....if................a rail strike?

Person B   ....catch the bus.

3 Person A   Where ....eat tonight?

Person B   ....Luigi's Italian restaurant.

Person A   What....................................full?

Person B   ....go to the Chinese

restaurant next door.

❼ **The world in 2025.** Think about the future. What will it be like? Use the prompts to write down your ideas.

1 I _____

2 I/live in _____

3 Computers _____

4 The air we breathe_____

5 Zoos_____

6 America_____

7 Jobs _____

8 Robots _____

9 Cars _____

10 Television _____

❽ Use the correct prepositions to complete the sentences.

1 The train leaves from Platform 4 _____ 9.15 am.

2 I'll see you _____ Saturday.

3 The operation will be finished _____ less than an hour.

4 After the course, I will stay in London _____ three days.

5 I'm flying home _____ 13th September.

❾ Choose appropriate verbs to complete the sentences.

1 I am ....to go on holiday to Thailand next year.
2 I .... to go to university to study medicine when I finish school.
3 I .... to become a doctor.
4 We .... her to arrive on the 9.15 train from Paddington Station.
5 They .... it will be better next year.

❿ Use the prompts to make statements and questions.

1 Why/not/come/to theatre?
2 What/do/if/miss/plane?
3 There/be/world peace/2025.
4 I/not/ever/understand/English grammar.
5 I/never/understand/English grammar.
6 She/plan/go/Greece/September.
7 I/not/got/any money/so/not/take/holiday/this summer.
8 Why/you/not/help me?
9 This car/so old/not/pass/road safety test.
10 I expect/go on learning/English/all my life.

⓫ Use the space below to write a paragraph about your future plans and intentions. Use the following verbs:

think   want   hope   plan   expect

Unit 4

83

COURSE DIARY

UNIT ONE • ASKING QUESTIONS

Date:_____

● What do you want to learn from this course? Complete the following chart:

grammar	vocabulary	pronunciation	British life
Examples ● talking about the past and the future	● the weather	● vowel sounds	● how to sound polite

● Think back over your first week in Britain. What questions can you remember? Use the space below to write them down.

other people's questions to you	your questions to other people

ACTION POINTS

● _____

● _____

● _____

LANGUAGE NOTEBOOK

Vocabulary

_____

_____

_____

_____

_____

_____

_____

_____

Useful expressions

_____

_____

_____

_____

_____

_____

_____

_____

Grammar points

_____

_____

_____

_____

_____

_____

_____

_____

_____

Course Diary

UNIT TWO • GETTING ABOUT

Date:_____

- You are now halfway through your course. Think back over your lessons. Look at your homework.
  How did you feel about your English when you first arrived? How do you feel now?
  What did you find difficult before? What do you find easier now? What do you still find quite difficult?

	listening	speaking	reading	writing
easier now				
still quite difficult				

- Think about the things you saw and heard during your first few days in Britain.
  What was the same as in your country? What was different? Write a few sentences.

_____

_____

_____

ACTION POINTS

- _____
- _____
- _____
- _____

LANGUAGE NOTEBOOK

Vocabulary

_____

_____

_____

_____

_____

_____

_____

_____

Useful expressions

_____

_____

_____

_____

_____

_____

_____

_____

_____

Grammar points

_____

_____

_____

_____

_____

_____

_____

_____

_____

UNIT THREE • MEETING PEOPLE

Date:_____

- Think about the British people you have met in the last few weeks. Read the following questions and write your answers.

  - Where did you meet them? Describe the place and the situation. (What was happening? What were they doing? What were you doing?)

    _____

    _____

    _____

    _____

  - Could you understand them? If not, why not?

    _____

    _____

    _____

    _____

  - Were they friendly and polite? Give some examples of the things they did and the things they said.

    _____

    _____

    _____

    _____

    _____

  - What did you notice about their English? Did they speak in the same way as your teachers, or differently?

    _____

    _____

    _____

    _____

  - What did you tell them about your country? What did they already know?

    _____

    _____

    _____

    _____

ACTION POINTS

- _____
- _____
- _____

LANGUAGE NOTEBOOK

Vocabulary

_____
_____
_____
_____
_____
_____
_____
_____

Useful expressions

_____
_____
_____
_____
_____
_____
_____
_____

Grammar points

_____
_____
_____
_____
_____
_____
_____

Course Diary

UNIT FOUR • PLANNING AHEAD

Date:_____

● Now that you are nearly at the end of your course, it is time to look back over the last few weeks...and to look ahead. Write your answers to the following questions. You can write as much or as little as you wish.

- What are the most interesting things that you have learned during the course?

_____
_____
_____
_____
_____

- What did you enjoy doing out of the classroom?

_____
_____
_____
_____
_____

- Was there anything that you did not enjoy?

_____
_____
_____
_____
_____

- Which parts of this book did you enjoy the most?   Which parts did you not like?

_____
_____
_____
_____
_____

ACTION POINTS

● _____
● _____
● _____
● _____

LANGUAGE NOTEBOOK

Vocabulary

Useful expressions

Grammar points

Course Diary

THE SOUNDS OF ENGLISH

Add your own examples in the spaces below:

Basic vowel sounds

/iː/ as in tea; free; magazine
_____

/ɪ/ as in information
_____

/e/ as in next; breakfast
_____

/æ/ as in bank
_____

/ə/ as in butcher;
_____

/ɜː/ as in birthday
_____

/ʌ/ as in London; bus
_____

/uː/ as in food
_____

/ʊ/ as in football; butcher
_____

/ɒ/ as in Oxford
_____

/ɔː/ as in store
_____

/aː/ as in department
_____

Double vowel sounds

/aɪ/ as in directory
_____

/ʊə/ as in tourist
_____

/ɔɪ/ as in enjoy; point
_____

/eɪ/ as in situation; Spain
_____

/əʊ/ as in postcard; slow
_____

/eə/ as in airline
_____

/ɪə/ as in sphere
_____
_____

Consonants

/b/ as in habits
_____

/g/ as in great
_____

/t/ as in television
_____

/f/ as in free; telephone
_____

/s/ as in sweater
_____

/θ/ as in theatre
_____

/ʃ/ as in shopping
_____

/tʃ/ as in church
_____

/m/ as in uniform
_____

/l/ as in policeman
_____

/h/ as in horrible
_____

/j/ as in yellow; university
_____

/p/ as in sport
_____

/k/ as in career; make; back
_____

/d/ as in directory
_____

/v/ as in positive
_____

/z/ as in magazine; trains
_____

/ð/ as in weather
_____

/ʒ/ as in television
_____

/dʒ/ as in judge
_____

/n/ as in teenager
_____

/r/ as in religion
_____

/w/ as in weather
_____

/ŋ/ as in interesting
_____

USEFUL EXPRESSIONS

Unit 1
Phrases and expressions
at least   1.1
Can you help me?   1.1
Certainly   1.1
Do take a seat   1.3
Don't worry   1.3
exactly   1.3
Excuse me   1.1
Fine   1.3
Fine, thanks   1.3
For example   1.3
Good   1.3
Good morning   1.1
Good to see you   1.3
Goodbye   1.1
Haven't seen you for ages   1.3
Hello!   1.3
Hey!   1.1
Hi!   1.3
How about...?   1.3
How are things going?   1.3
How are you?   1.3
How are you doing?   1.3
How are you getting on?   1.3
How do you do?   1.3
How nice to see you   1.3
How's it going?   1.3
I can't stand (it)   1.5
I'm afraid   1.1
I'm afraid not   1.3
I'm pleased to meet you   1.3
I'm sorry   1.1
Is that all right with you?   1.3
It's getting late   1.5
nice to have met you   1.3
nice to see you again   1.3
Not too bad   1.3
Of course   1.1
OK   1.3
only   1.3
please   1.1
really   1.1
Sorry   1.8
Sorry I'm a bit late   1.3
Sure   1.3
Thank you   1.3
Thanks   1.3
Thanks very much   1.1
That's OK   1.3
Turn left   1.3
usually   1.3
What about you?   1.4
What's new?   1.3
Welcome   1.6

Unit 2
Phrases and expressions
All right   2.4

Can I help you?   2.1
Can you give me...?   2.3
Can you help me?   2.1
Certainly   2.3
Could I have the bill?   2.3
Could you give me...?   2.3
Could you tell me the time?   2.3
Don't mention it   2.6
Don't worry   2.2
Don't worry about it   2.6
Excuse me   2.1
Fancy a drink?   2.4
Fine   2.4
Give us a hand   2.3
Good morning   2.1
Great   2.1
Hello   2.1
Help!   2.3
Here it is   2.1
How about (+ -ing)?   2.4
I don't know   2.1
I was wondering if (+ would)   2.4
I wonder if I could possibly trouble you for   2.3
I wonder if you could give me   2.3
I wonder if you could possibly give me   2.3
I'd better (+ verb)   2.2
I'd love to   2.6
I'm after (= I'm looking for)   2.1
I'm sorry   2.2
I'm sorry to bother you   2.6
I'm terribly sorry   2.6
I've been on my feet all day   2.4
It's nothing   2.6
Let's (+ verb)   2.4
Morning!   2.2
No, thank you   2.2
No thanks   2.4
Not at all   2.6
of course   2.4
One thing at a time   2.4
please   2.1
Please could you give me   2.3
Right   2.1
She's expecting you   2.1
Sure   2.3
Take the (first, second) on the left/right   2.1
Thank you   2.1
Thank you very much   2.6
Thanks   2.1
Thanks, anyway   2.2
That's just what I wanted   2.6
That's very kind of you   2.6
Tickets, please!   2.2
We haven't got any left   2.2
What's it doing (there)?   2.1
Yes, certainly   2.1
Yes, of course   2.2
Yes, please   2.6

Unit 3
Phrases and expressions
Bye 3.3
Bye bye 3.3
Bye for now 3.3
Cheerio 3.3
Cheers! 3.3
(You must) come again soon 3.3
darling 3.2
Excuse me 3.1
Get out of my hair! 3.4
Glad you could come 3.3
Good evening 3.1
Goodbye 3.3
Great evening 3.3
Have you been waiting long? 3.2
Hello 3.8
Here we are 3.1
Hi! 3.8
How would you like it? 3.1
How are you? 3.8
How would that suit you? 3.1
How's life with you? 3.8
I do hope you can come and see us again soon 3.3
I don't care 3.6
I don't know 3.1
I had a great time 3.3
I must go 3.3
I see 3.8
I (really) think (I'd/we'd) better be going 3.3
I wonder if I could (+ verb) 3.7
I'm not sure 3.1
I'm sorry 3.3
Is that the time? 3.3
It was a pleasure 3.3
It was a wonderful evening 3.3
It was nice to see you again 3.8
It was very kind of you to invite me 3.3
It's getting (rather) late 3.3
It's time to go 3.3
It's time we went 3.3
It's time we were going 3.3
Leave me alone! 3.4
Look! 3.4
(I/We) must be going 3.3
My idea of (+ noun) 3.6
Not going, are you? 3.3
Oh, by the way... 3.8
Oh, I see 3.2
Oh, is that the time? 3.8
OK 3.3
please 3.1
(I/We) really should be going 3.3
See you later 3.3
See you 3.3
See you soon, I hope 3.8
Sorry 3.2
Sorry? 3.8
Sorry to break up the party 3.3
Take care 3.3
Thank you 3.1
Thank you for inviting me 3.3
Thank you once again 3.3
Thank you so much 3.3

Thank you very much 3.3
Thanks a lot 3.3
Thanks for (the party) 3.3
That reminds me... 3.8
That's OK 3.3
That's right 3.1
That's (very) kind of you 3.3
That's very true 3.8
There you are 3.1
Time to go 3.3
We must meet again soon 3.8
What about...? 3.8
What are you doing these days? 3.8
What have you been doing lately? 3.8
What time do you think it is? 3.2
Where on earth have you been? 3.2
Will it take long? 3.2
You don't have to leave yet, do you? 3.3
You're welcome 3.3

Unit 4
Phrases and expressions
Above all else 4.1
'Bye for now 4.5
Can you pass me the salt, please? 4.7
darling 4.2
How was your evening/weekend? 4.1
I didn't care for it very much 4.2
I don't know 4.4
I quite liked it 4.2
I suppose 4.2
I wasn't too keen on it 4.2
I'll be back 4.5
I'll see you soon 4.4
I'm afraid 4.2
I'm going to wait and see what turns up 4.5
I'm not sure 4.5
In fact 4.1
It was fairly good 4.2
It was OK 4.2
It was rather good, actually 4.2
It wasn't really my kind of thing 4.2
It wasn't terribly good 4.2
It wasn't too bad at all 4.2
Maybe I will - maybe I won't 4.4
of course 4.5
Please give them my apologies 4.5
Really? 4.2
Sorry about that 4.1
That's it 4.5
That's not all 4.1
What happened to you? 4.1
What was it like? 4.1
you know 4.1